Powell Street Diary

By Jesse Hideo Nishihata

Disclaimer

This work is a posthumous diary and thus, while it is based on true events, it is subject to lapses in memory, whether selective or unintentional. The publisher claims no responsibility for any misrepresentations or incorrect dates, etc., as these were events lived by the author and set on the page many years following the initial event. Likewise, the author's use of language has been untouched; there may be occasional uses of words and phrases that may offend some readers.

This work was previously published in Pan-Japan, Volume 1, Number 1, Spring 2000, by Illinois State University.

© 2017 Jesse Nishihata. All rights reserved.
ISBN 978-1-387-09174-4 (ebook)

Published by Tombo Communications, Montreal, Canada

Foreword

There's a story my father Jesse used to tell about the origins of our family name, Nishihata. Our Japanese roots are in Shiga prefecture in the Kansai area, not far from Kyoto, in a little town called Echigawa[1]. The town sits in a broad floodplain, punctuated by the occasional short, steep mountain. Typical Japanese topography, in other words. It's also reputed to be filled with ghosts, as it was often at the centre of the multiple battles that went on during the Sengoku period of Japanese history, when the country was in a state of civil war for almost a century.

The adoption of surnames in Japan was relatively recent, only beginning in 1875 following a law that was issued by the Meiji-era government. Prior to this, surnames had been forbidden to the peasantry, as it was a mark of distinction that only the samurai class and above were entitled to. So when the new law passed, a lot of families had to improvise, or consult with their local priest to come up with an acceptable family moniker.

The name Nishihata is made up of two kanji characters, nishi (西) meaning west and hata (畑), which itself is composed of two radical characters, ka (火) for fire and ta (田) for field, or field burn. Through Jesse's logic, the fact that we were associated with burning fields in the West meant that our family at one point were clearing land, which implied to him that his ancestors had only recently come into property. He would

---

[1] As an interesting aside, the characters for Echigawa (愛知川) transliterate as 'knowing love river'

sum it all up by saying to us, "oh, we were just newcomers," in a sheepish and resigned tone of voice.

Although I lived in Japan and even went back to our ancestral seat in Shiga, I never found out if his hunch was correct. But I began to suspect he did not base this theory on any research, but rather a deep-seated diffidence over his Japanese identity. And so, my own theory is that this feeling of embarrassment, of being out of place even in his parents' homeland, is a result of the Internment experience.

I am sure many of you are familiar with the broad outlines of Internment, of how more than 20,000 Japanese-Canadians were dispossessed of their rights, their lands, and virtually everything else that they could not carry with their own hands, and sent off to live in concentration camps (which as a term has strong associations, but is accurate as the camps they lived in for the war years were concentrations of people with Japanese and no other ancestry) until the end of the war. Afterward, they were told to either get out of the country altogether or to scatter across the country settling again anywhere - except where many of them had been born and grew up, which included Jesse.

Having grown up in the shadow of this event, I am convinced that the systematic deconstruction of the Japanese identity by the various levels of the Canadian government of the time resulted in much more than just some kind of forced transfer of economic assets. It was like a vivisection of a human heart, a tearing away of meaning and hope, and all done without violence. I have long believed that the Interment experience in the Canadian context was a kind of 'double-whammy' in that the innate politeness of the Japanese, combined with the ostensible gentility of the primarily white authorities made natural rage or anger an impossibility. Which leaves the survivors (for want of a better word) of the incident ill-equipped to actively respond to any of it. Hence the decades of repression, guilt and denial. As a burden, it has taken time to define its size, shape and weight. And yet it has been present for many of us, for many years.

Through all this Powell Street, which was the center of Vancouver's Japantown, and where Jesse himself was born, remained his spiritual home. Years later, when he was suffering from Alzheimer's disease, he took to wandering, as do many people who suffer from that horrible illness. He took to wandering so far that we got a call one night from the Peel Regional police force, who explained they had picked him up in Mississauga. It was about 30 kilometres from his home in Toronto. "I've got to go to Vancouver," Jesse said when he came back home, safe and sound thankfully. Significantly, he was headed due west. On foot.

The genesis of this diary is also somewhat circuitous, as it is not a true diary per se, but a recollection after that fact. It began as a treatment for a possible TV series, which had the working title "Little Tokyo." A friend of Jesse's in the film business proposed the idea to him, and asked him to write something that would evoke life back in those days on Powell Street. So at the age of 50-something, Jesse re-imagined and relived his days as a twelve-year-old growing up on that particular stretch of road by Oppenheimer Park in downtown Vancouver.

What is remarkable in this work is the intensity of detail, and the vivid descriptions of daily living in a bygone era. If you ever wanted to learn the rules for marbles, here is your chance. He brings to life the time before the war, along with the uncertainties and confusion that arise as the war plays out, along with the various orders and proclamations that began to ship people off, until finally, Jesse and his family are given their orders to leave as well. Indeed, 2017 marks the 75th anniversary of that day, and thus an ideal time to release this work, which will hopefully spur others to understand the impact that this dislocation had upon thousands of families.

The other effective aspect of this book is how well Jesse portrays himself, which may seem an odd thing to say, since it is a diary. However, a number of people who read the diary commented that the language seems rather mature for a twelve-year-old boy. But he was no ordinary preteen, just as Jesse was no ordinary man. In the phrasings and perspectives he presents, we can see the tremendous intelligence that would emerge in his adult life. If there is one imprint I have of my father, it is that: his power of thought and his insight. He was always concerned with determining what was the truth of a given situation, and never took things at face value.

It bears explaining that Jesse was not always known by this name. At birth he was called Hideo by his parents, with Kanji characters 英夫 that meant 'brave man.' It was during his Internment at Tashme near Hope, BC that he took the name Jesse, as part of his conversion to Christianity. Jesse was the name of one of the moderators of the United Church, who were providing education to the camp. Although later in life he did not remain a devout Christian, he seemed to inhabit his adopted name in a more total way. Everyone knew him as Jesse; only his mother stuck to calling him Hideo.

When I first read this diary, I was struck by the impression that it is not so much a book about the Japanese-Canadian experience, as it is about a boy growing up, albeit in troubled times. A boy trying to piece together what is happening inside of him, as much as what is going on around him. In this sense, I found it similar to the Diary of Anne Frank which I also recall was extremely personal, despite the event in which it is embedded. Nevertheless, it gives a weight to history that simple textbooks cannot convey. So it is with the Powell Street Diary. It shows us that in the end, our most important struggles are not always the ones that sweep up the greatest numbers of people, or that pit nations against each other, or themselves. The most important struggles are the very small ones inside of each of us, the ones that cannot be seen or felt by others, but which are nonetheless felt very, very deeply.

Junji Nishihata, 2017

Biography

JESSE HIDEO NISHIHATA (1929-2006) was a pioneer in Japanese Canadian documentary filmmaking. From 1966-1978 Jesse worked as a contract producer for the CBC-TV Public Affairs Department. During this time Jesse produced and directed numerous documentaries including such films as Watari Dori: A Bird of Passage (1973). Watari Dori uses Jesse's own family history as a framework for exploring the Japanese Canadian internment. This was the first film concerning the Japanese Canadian World War II experience to be broadcast on Canadian television.

From 1979-1995, Jesse taught film and media studies at Ryerson University's Image Arts department. It was during this period that Jesse established himself as an independent producer and director.

Jesse's independent productions include some of his most seminal works such as The Inquiry Film (1977). This film provides a visual report of the commission of Inquiry conducted by Mr. Justice Thomas R. Berger into the social, economic and environmental impact of a proposed pipeline in the Western Arctic region known as the Mackenzie Valley.

The Inquiry Film earned Jesse the 1977 Canadian Film Award (now know as the Genie Award) for Best Documentary over 60 minutes and the Golden Athena for Best Feature Documentary at the 1978 Athens international Film Festival in Ohio.

Jesse also ventured into the avant-garde through films such as Black Earth (1988), an experimental visual-essay, which illustrates a poetic metaphor of the earth as a woman. Black Earth was filmed on location in India and was awarded a citation for Personal Vision and Cinematography at the 1988 Oakland International Film Festival.

Other notable films include Justice in Our Time: how Redress was won (1989), a video record of the Japanese Canadian fight for Redress and Catch the Spirit! (1991), which documents the Earth Spirit Festival.

Acknowledgements

I would be remiss not to mention the many people who have contributed to the re-publication of this diary. Their time, effort and advice helped me bring this project to fruition, after years and years of planning. I wish to thank my siblings Alexis, Akira, Masashi and Emmy, my wife Akiko and my children Shu, Koko and Gen. They have all provided the emotional support necessary to get this book off the ground. Thank you.

A special thank you to my uncle Shoji who is the last surviving member of the family portrayed in these pages. He still believes that the history of the Japanese-Canadians is not understood well enough by most people in this country. I hope this book will help address that gap.

And warm thanks to all the readers, editors and collaborators whom I name here in no particular order: Jane Marvy, Norm Ibuki, Linda Cartwright, Alan Itakura, Dave Nishihata, Paul Nishihata, Emiko Morita, Leanne Dunic, Sally Ito, Sherri Kajiwara, Mike Murakami, Yukio Koglin, Peter Farbridge, Kyo Maclear and Nobuko Adachi.

Thursday, November 20, 1941 - Today is my birthday and I got the best present ever, a wrist watch! It's Swiss made, with a 17-jewel movement, and luminous hands and numbers so you can see the time in the dark, and a black leather strap. And a nice round stainless steel casing. I look at it every time. Flicking my left wrist over, watching the second hand sweep around, and comparing it to the big clock in the shop, and seeing whether the second hands move at the same time. I take it off and put it on, just to feel the doing of it. And I've broken it already. I kept on winding and winding it, and I broke the winder. But Tak said it could be easily replaced at Mc & Mc[1], where Papa got it, and it will be brand new again. Mama is upset that I don't take care of things. She doesn't know how much I want to keep touching it and doing things with it. Like winding it up. Papa just said be careful next time.

So today is my birthday and I am twelve years old; next year I will be thirteen. That already sounds old. According to Mama's count, I'm there already. How does that work out? Mama's present is this diary book. She said a diary can be your very best friend. She said it doesn't matter how or where or when you start. You just do it and let it grow, she said. So here I am. This isn't the first time I'm keeping a diary. When I was a *san-nen-sei*[2] in the Japanese School, Mrs. Tanaka, our teacher gave us a

---

1 A popular hardware store
2 A third grade student

nikki[3] and we all had to keep it going for one whole year, in Japanese. It isn't the same now. It doesn't feel so dutiful. It's on my own now. I know my entries were pretty limited then: the weather, rain or shine, get up

Left to right: Sumi, Miyo, Hideo (me), Shoji

---

3 A diary

time and bed time, and whether it was a school day or not, that sort of thing. Nothing very useful to anyone. I look at it now, and think, how childish? Except for that one big occasion when Prince Chichibu and his Princess visited Vancouver on their way to the Coronation in London, and came to the Gogakko. I was really thrilled to know that they would visit our classroom and see our schoolwork on the wall, and maybe even my composition work, which Tanaka-sensei said was one of the best. I wrote about that and about waving two flags that day. And here it is, a whole page about that on that day, October 17, 1937! Very plain, very simple. In Japanese!

But it's odd to start a diary so late in the year. Not according to Mama though: "*Ii, tanjobi dakara...* It's your birthday, an auspicious time. A good time to start," she said. And so, today, a watch and a diary. And a crisp new dollar bill from Tak. He gave it to me when nobody was looking. Just between us, he said.

Saturday, November 22, 1941 - I've been thinking about this diary business. Does it have to be everyday? And exactly what do I write about? The dictionary says: "from 'diarium,' Latin, 'a daily allowance'; a daily written record, especially of the writer's own experiences, thoughts, etc." And "experience, and actual living through an event or events, personally undergoing or observing something or things in general as they occur."

It's true, I don't tell anybody everything that happens to me or think about. It's impossible! Not even your best friend. Best friend? Well, seriously, do I have a best friend? I am talking to myself; in the same way do I write to myself? Sure, so I can see in the future what happened to me now. So that's it, then.

Let's start by bringing things up to date. I was born twelve years ago in 1929 in Vancouver, B.C. and right now I live at 457 Powell Street with my parents and two younger sisters and one younger brother. I am the oldest. My father's name is Saburo, and my mother's, Kishi, but we never ever call them by their names. Papa and Mama, that's all. Other kids call their parents, Tochan and Kaa-chan in the Japanese way, but us, never. We are spaced two years apart, and we go boy, girl, boy, girl, and the names are: Hide (that's me), Miyo, Shoji and Sumi. Papa was born in 1898, and Mama in 1909. They come from the same village in Shiga-ken, Japan; a place called Echigawa, which is near Biwa Lake, not far from Kyoto.

Mama tells me all these things, Papa has never said anything about them. But actually she tells more about Japan and things Japanese to Rinzo Amemori, the good Japanese school student next door, when it's New Year's Day or something and he is over with his sister, and they are looking through our family album. But I'm sure Mama intends me to hear these stories by the way she looks at me as I cup my face with my hands, both elbows on the table, mouth slightly open, or filled with manju.

Rinzo works at the Japanese newspaper, Tairiku Nippo, The Continental Times. I don't know exactly what he does there, but he is certainly good in Japanese and really interested and laps up everything about Japan that Mama tells him. I think of Japan as the place where Mama and Papa come from, that's all. Not as any place special for me. But Mama has a brother in the Japanese Navy, and there is a good strong picture of him in his navy uniform, and an even better one of him on a rattan chair in a hospital dressing gown and a puffy white cap with a naval insignia. And then there's the large framed picture of the battle cruiser he serves on. And can I ever look at those pictures! All day!

Papa is a tinsmith and has his own sheet metal shop. He learnt the trade as an apprentice at the Akiyama Hardware Store; also roomed and boarded and was just like a member of that family. All his friends and hobbies come from that time. Like Mr. Miyasaki and Shiraishi-san, and fishing and snappy clothes. Mr. Miyasaki, "Oji-san" we'd call him, but then every older man was automatically an oji-san, and a woman was an oba-san. It's like calling all the adults either uncle or aunt. It's late now. Tomorrow, off to fishing on the sandbars of the Fraser with Papa. He said we'll go to Mission, and row across the island in the river. Have to get up early, so this is it.

Papa in front of his shop.

Monday, November 24, 1941 - For supper we had the trouts we caught yesterday including the one I got myself. Last night I was too tired to write down anything. We came home late, Papa's truck sort of crept along the highway, heavy fog and much traffic. The tail lights ahead blinking each time the brakes are put on. Blinking red lights snaking out in the dark. In this truck, an International Harvester van with a long body, I sit on an apple crate behind Papa, the driver. Mr. Aoki, who came with us, sat in the other seat in front. His son, Mikio, a solemn guy with glasses, sits like me on a crate behind him. They are not much fun; they're stuffy.

But I like it out in the early morning and the river with the mist rising; I like the bonfire and the sandwich lunch with thermos tea, and the silent watching of the river. Deep and wide. The Fraser must be half a mile wide at Mission, and the deep currents have a strong pull to them.

We do still-fishing: you cast or throw the line with a lead sinker at the end and a gang of fish hooks baited with cooked salmon eggs; you tighten the line and prop the rod on a stick and wait for the fish to bite. When it does, the bell at the end of the rod jingles; then you pick up the rod or the line and wait until you feel the fish tug at the bait... you let out the line a bit, and then you pull a nice tug and hook the fish, and you pull him in with the line or reel him in with the rod. Still fishing.

Monday. School. Strathcona School, out on Pender and Jackson. Our motto is: "The school with many nationalities but only one flag." But sometimes you'd think it's only one nationality, the Japanese! I'm in Grade Seven. Next year, it's Grade Eight, and we'll have to think about what do we do after Strathcona. But nobody's doing any of that now. Our teacher's name is Miss Bolton. She is stiff and very English. In our class we sit in order of rank, how well we do in our tests. The desk for the head of the class which is at the front of the first row on the right side of the class is usually occupied by Victor Shimizu, son of the United Church minister at the Powell and Jackson Street Church. The second seat is occupied by Evelyn Chin, our 'aristocratic' Chinese girl: she looks so severe, always. In September it was the other way around, Evelyn in the front desk and Victor in the second. After that it's Dawn Wren. I sit in the second row near the front, but once I had a desk in the first row near the back. But in this seat now I am diagonally almost behind Dawn, and I can have a good look at her. I guess she's half English or something, the Chinese part of her is her eyes and cheeks and hair, but she's what you'd call "fair." Sometimes her mouth falls open. I really like her name, Dawn Wren.

Behind Dawn is Michiko Ishii, the eager beaver, eager to please, always on the get up and go, the first to volunteer for anything. She sits opposite me. This rank order business can be awful. After a big test in everything, we all have to get out of our desk and line up along the blackboard walls and wait for Miss Bolton to assign us our seats, according to how we performed. What a big thing! I'm so relieved when my name is called and I slide into my seat in humiliation and pride. What about Toivo near the end of the last row, the far row in the classroom? He looks unconcerned. Toivo Rantella, that's another name! He's blond blond, almost white blond.

It's starting to rain out in the dark night. I'm tired.

Wednesday, November 26, 1941 - Just came back from the Gym; "Harry's Cleaners" were practising. Okay, the Gym is the gymnasium of the Powell Street Japanese United Church and it's usually called the Japanese Gym. That's the place where they play basketball games and where there's the spiral street staircase at one end of the court on which I like to go up and down from the floor to the wall balcony that rings the court. Joe Akiyama was out there charging up the "Harry's Cleaners" team. He's the top centre in the league. On Friday night they play against Marpole, and then on Saturday night, it's a home game at the Gym against Kitsilano. Joe's a swell guy but in the game you'd never know; he's fierce. He plays it real hard, watching him you'd get excited and nervous. He's so restless. Always moving. Even at practising. Snapping at everybody. But Sockeye Tsukamoto, the shortest on the team, who's just as aggressive as Joe, doesn't look mad all the time. Joe plays so hard it's more than a basketball game.

Afterwards, he asked after Papa: "How's Cha-chan?" I showed him my wrist watch. Tak had taken it back to Mc & Mc and got it fixed. Joe looked real close at it but I lost him to a small bubble of friends, guys and girls. And tonight it's foggy and you can hear the fog horns in the harbour.

Saturday, November 29, 1941 - This is the first time I'm writing about a Saturday. I was up like a shot. Cleaned up the front of the *mise*, the shop, swept it up and the shop floor, and then went on to the library at Hastings and Main, on roller skates. People are scared to see kids like me coming at them on roller skates; some just stand still, other scowl or make faces of annoyance. I like dodging among the people and things and the tingle of the vibrations of the skates on my feet.

At the library, I have a reading plan: I'm going to take out every book in the biography section, going right through the whole stack that's on one end of the library. Not too methodically. Last week I jumped from F to L and took out one on Joseph Lister, an English medical doctor in the late nineteenth century who brought about extended antiseptic procedures in London hospitals and improved surgical practices. Now he's just a name for a gargle, "Listerine." Then, today, I jumped to W and took out one on James Watt, inventor of steam engines. At the library, met up with Junpei Hatashima, same grade at Strathcona but not in the same class, but in the same grade and glass at the Japanese School. He likes to look at Jane's All the Fighting Ships in the Reference Section, and together we pored over the British battleships, again. Especially "HMS Prince of Wales," just launched in 1939. Not too much about Japanese ships, but we always look for the flagship of the Imperial Japanese Navy, the battleship "Mutsu" which we agree cannot compare with HMS Prince of Wales because it has this pagoda tiered superstructure, about which we agree that it has too high a silhouette, making an easy target for a submarine, and is not as fast as the British ship. Junpei, or Thomas as he is also known, likes everything about the sea and the navy. I've told him about Mama's brother, and about the pictures. Maybe one day I'll let him come over and have a good look at the battle cruiser.

In the afternoon, I hopped on the bar of Tak's bike and went with him on his round of account collecting. We called on people's houses mostly, but sometimes stores and machine shops. I'd watch the bike as Tak went in and did his business. We went as far as Heatley Avenue and the Heaps and even made one call in Chinatown. Sometimes Tak explained what the accounts were for, like that one at the Chinese store on Pender Street, it was for a fish tank. But mostly he talked about the movie he saw the other night with his girl friend, Jean, at the Orpheum, "Maltese Falcon" starring Humphrey Bogart. I couldn't follow the story, but I listened. Then he talked about his girlfriend, Jean, and said what a swell gal she is, a real sweetheart. She's seventeen. Only five years older than me. And Tak said: "Don't worry, Spike, you'll have a girl friend soon enough." And then at Ohori's we had a milk shake. After supper, went to see the basketball game at the Gym; Joe played so roughly he was defaulted out of the game. But even so he was the top scorer. He is so intense; he plays with his eyes blazing. People are really wild about him, one way or another.

Early rising tomorrow. Going fishing with the Miyasaki's, Freddy and his Dad, in their passenger car, a 4-door Chevrolet. Mr. Miyasaki, Shigeru-san, Papa calls him, is an old, old friend of Papa. Unlike him though, Mr. Miyasaki was born in Vancouver, so he is a Nisei, and so is his wife. They have two other boys, Richard, same age as Miyo, and Kenny, about the same age as Sumi. And they have Ba-chan, Mr. Miyasaki's mother, too. And they all live on Davies Street, out on English Bay, where they run a dry cleaning shop, and live behind the shop. There are three or four other Japanese families out around that way, and of course they all know each other.

Our two families have been going out for picnics and things like that ever since I can remember, and sometimes with Papa's other friends and their families, a whole crowd, out to Lynn Creek and Jericho Beach, and Bowen Sound. But last summer we couldn't picnic at Jericho Beach anymore because Japan had done something. Japs? I guess we are Japanese.

Ladner tomorrow, on the south banks.

Monday, December 1, 1941 - Japanese school: it's funny the things you learn at Japanese school. I remember the story about Columbus and the egg. It seems he was a practical guy. Once when asked to stand an egg on its end after all others had tried and failed, he took the egg and chipped it at the end, and made it stand. It made an impression on me. It was a story in our language text book. Nowadays, the text books are cut up and some pages are taken out. Akiyama-sensei never bothered to explain, but Mama said it was probably because there was something that the people here did not like. Wonder what was taken out.

His classes are much more strict than at Strathcona, and we are always told to do better than we can. Freddie does very well and his mom and dad are proud of him. He is a yutosei, an honour student. Without doing anything, I'm jealous of him, and I think that he's just doing it to look good to his parents.

When I'm at their place he hardly ever talks to them in Japanese, even to Ba-chan. But he keeps up his homework, and there is plenty of that. I'm always being scolded about it 'cause I don't do it. He and Richard, his brother, and their friend Eddie Morita come all the way over from English Bay on the streetcar and go all the way back home after school on the street car. Akiyama-sensei! Respect for old people, parents and teachers is drilled well into our heads in his class and he enforces this with his reputation as a kendo teacher. But we all him Hackenbush after the Groucho Marx character because he has that brush moustache and the funny walk. He lives at the school, over in the older wooden building. I guess he's married to the school. He gets very poetic when he talks about the Meiji Tenno, the emperor who brought about the modern era in Japan with a strong grasp of old traditional values. Akiyama-sensei likes to go over Meiji Tenno's poems in great detail and he manages to make them sound like sermons. I guess there's something religious about them, but plainly understood, they are moving. There is one about how your heart should be as clear as the mirror that reflects your image in the morning.

There's no doubt that Akiyama-sensei is proud to be Japanese.

I think about the teachers at Strathcona and I feel they don't shine the way he does, but I recall the Remembrance Day assembly a couple of weeks ago at the school auditorium when there was something. Maybe it was just the singing of "In Flander's Fields" by the whole school or the way Miss Nelson told the story of Edith Cavell, the nurse executed by the Germans in the Great War, but that sense of pride was held by everyone; it was something you could touch. Is this patriotism? Well, I feel it like that when we are told stories about the Battle of Britain and are asked to join in and help the embattled English people in their little island kingdom; and we do and did, through and through with the SOSL, the Strathcona Overseas Service League. Made it sound so grown up, and us along with it. We really believe that "There'll Always be an England." But I guess the main thing is that we want to go along with everybody else. I do. It doesn't matter that almost all of the class is us Japanese kids; we all feel the same. I can poke at Rosie and pull her blonde braids when we line up at the front blackboard for the spelling contest, and she raises up and throws her hands down and sharply whispers, "Oh, Heeddeo!" and turns around and gives me a smile.

But we also do other funny things at school, like marching around like soldiers during our phys-ed period. Mr. Chappelle, the gym teacher hup-hup-hupping us along, and trying to teach us complicated marching drills, like whole rank wheeling, maneuvers, he called them. Junji Kinoshita, the little shrimp and Mr. Chappelle's pet, would be the pivot marcher, as the whole line wheeled about him, from a file to a line and then made a snap turn to the left and marched along again as a column. Even here we get into the spirit of the thing and bump along. I guess the high point was this year's May Day sports ceremony when the boys marched down to Powell Grounds in file columns and wheeled smartly into rank formation and advanced in three lines across the breadth of the field and came to a halt in front of the inspection party. That month the whole city seemed to be excited about the war and wartime practices because there were the air raid siren drills and blackout exercises. It made me feel connected with things. By doing things together I belonged with everyone. "We'll all pull together through the stormy weather, carry on, carry on, carry on...." So goes the song.

If I go to war, I want to be in the Navy! The Senior Service. Or maybe, the RAF! In a Hurricane! But, yes the Navy: "For there's something about a sailor, well you know what sailors are. Bright and breezy, free and easy, he's the ladies' pride and joy. Falls in love with Kate and Jane, then he's off to sea again: ship ahoy, ship ahoy!" So goes the song.

Friday, December 5, 1941 - Scotty, Rinzo's brother, hurt his foot fooling around in the shop this evening. There's this big block of wood about 3' by 3' by 5', good and solid, used for bending things and as work table. In trying to pivot and turn it on one corner, Scotty lost his grip on the thing and it crashed on his foot. Had to cut his running shoe open, but it looks like no bones are broken. So says Rinzo who took him to the neighbourhood doctor, Dr. Uchida. Papa wasn't there, Tak had already gone home, but the side doors were open and the Amemori boys came in and fooled around. Just like Bill Tanaka, banging two hammers about one day last year, and a tiny, tiny chip of steel got into his eyes. No one knew about that. And now it looks as if he's going to lose sight in that eye. Accidents?

Mama really got angry with Rinzo. "You should know better," she said, "you must keep your wits about you. What would you do if you had a really big accident!" Rinzo looked so sheepish.

Sunday, December 7, 1941 - Something happened today, and I don't know what! The Japs bombed a place called Pearl Harbour and they say it's war! So let's start at the beginning. We heard about it on the car radio as we headed for home after the day's fishing at Mission banks. Japs bombed Pearl Harbour, an American Naval base in Hawaii. Mr. Miyasaki just couldn't believe it, he kept banging his hands on the wheels of his car, and slapping the dashboard, and turning to Papa and saying, "Oi Nishi, what do you think? Eh?" And Papa was saying it was bound to come the way things were going, but not like this. But they both thought that in the short run Japan might win. How? they didn't know. They smoked a lot of cigarettes as the car wound its way. Before the Second Narrows, across the waters, the lights at the Imperial Oil's refinery town spelled out its name, "IOCO." They joked that it might be a target. Freddie and I looked at each other, we were both strangely silent. It had been a long day. I guess we were both exhausted because both our kid brothers were along today, Richard and Shoji. Now they were both fast asleep. We think of them as real kids, and a nuisance. Maybe Richard not so much, but Shoji for sure. And then all day we had this huge bonfire going, fed by two big rubber tires. The fire coiled up in big black smoke and we all felt as if we'd done a bad thing when the game warden in his hip waders drifted by in the afternoon. He didn't even check for our fishing permits. He had an odd smile on his face. Maybe he knew, and wasn't telling us! "He must've known," says Mr. Miyasaki.

He wants to hurry home, but the traffic winds slow-fast through the now misty evening. At home there's a note saying Mama and the girls have gone over to the Miyasakis. By the time we get there we are all even more excited by the whole thing, and the grown ups buzz away amongst themselves in the front room as Freddie and I jabber away in his room. We are pilots in the RAF and are buzzing our own way! We shout: carry on, carry on, carry on! and fly about with outstretched arms! Phone rings! One of the calls is about a lighted kerosene lamp thrown into the hallway of Mr. Kamenishi's rooming house on Dunlevy and Alexander! We are driven back home by Oji-san, all subdued and very tired. There's a war on. A stab in the back, the radio said.

Monday, December 8, 1941 - School was very, very quiet today. It was as if we all spoke in whispers, even the teachers. In the sewing period I pricked my finger and cried out "ouch!" and somebody laughed. My eyes smarted and Miss Bolton came up and asked if I was all right. I hung my head and didn't reply. And it was grey all day. Only in Mr. Chappelle's period did it feel almost okay, because we barged about the gym tossing basketballs into the hoops and medicine balls at each other. No one got the strap for fooling around. When we got home we were told there'd be no more Japanese school. Gee, just like that, no more Japanese school.

I half-listened to Tak as he talked away about news from the war fronts; he was soldering a big water tank and I helped with the daubing of the acid and tending of the solder irons. Would he go fight in the war, I asked. He said, hell, no, he wouldn't fight for any side, besides they wouldn't take the Japanese into the services anyway. Some guys he knew had been trying to do just that, and he thought they were crazy. They couldn't get in. We're Japs, he said. "Peanuts" Koyanagi came by near closing time, and he and Tak walked off homeward after closing the shop. He walked the bike. It was early closing; there was going to be a blackout tonight. Earlier this year, in May, the city had a blackout practice and we all sat out then in Powell Grounds to see how it would turn out. It was generally thought that our Japtown did all right. All the lights were off or were blocked off. But out on the north shore in North Vancouver, a lot of lights were on, and we hooted and shouted. Tonight, it looks like for real. Mama has draped the windows with dark cloth and we are all kind of quiet. Mama as usual knitting sweaters, this time a cabled cardigan for Shoji. Mine is already done, a dark green one with a zippered front. She always does them by pairs. Papa comes home and says to Mama that some people have been picked up and are being held at the Immigration

Building. "Why?" asks Mama. Papa looks up from his game of solitaire and shrugs. Picked up by the Mounties. "Mounten Police" Mama calls them, as in mountain police. Were they on horsebacks or what, I want to know. Cars, says Papa. I ask: were you there? No, he says.

We live in the quarters behind the shop, but behind us there is the living space of the Nakamura family, all grown ups. There's Nancy and her sister Mary, and their brother, Eddy. They all go out to work. Nancy as a house-girl someplace in South Van and Eddy in a paper factory and Mary is a waitress in the restaurant where her father is a cook, and the mother in a laundry someplace. Sometimes in the evening their radio could be heard through the walls as Nancy and Mary laugh along to the Amos 'n' Andy Show, or Fibber Magee and Molly. Tonight, it's all very quiet. Maybe the radio is on a murmuring level. And upstairs, the Oyas. Mr. Oya, who works at the Japanese Consulate, and Mrs. Oya have three girls: Naomi, Miyo's friend, Ida, and Nana, the baby, Rita. They have a big living space, as big as the shop and our space together. Mr. Oya is skinny and Mrs. Oya is plump. Jack Sprat who ate no fat and his wife who ate no lean. They are both Niseis and English is the language in their house. It is said that Mr. Oya is the oldest Canadian-born person in the country. You could get on the history books for that. They own the building that houses the shop and our home and the Nakamura's at the back, and the Nabata Shoe Repairs next to us.

With that dollar from Taka-chan, I had bought a copy of "How Green Was My Valley" by Richard Llewellyn, and I continue to plow deeply through that book. I had seen the movie at the Orpheum with Freddie back in September, and I read the story now with a deeper sense of the people in the story, having seen Roddy McDowell as Huw and Maureen O'Hara as Astrahan, Huw's sister, and Walter Pidgeon as the Reverend, and Donald Crisp as the father, and Sara Allgood as the mother. And I am going back to them now, going back to Huw and Dai Bando, his boxing mentor.

Wednesday, December 10, 1941 - HMS Prince of Wales and HMS Repulse sunk by Japanese planes! Unbelievable! What's next? No more fishing trips on Sunday, for sure.

Saturday, December 20, 1941 - Last day of school yesterday, and in the afternoon, a Christmas pageant in the auditorium. Christmas carols, and a recitation of "'Twas the Last Day of Christmas," and again, the acting out of "Good King Wenceslas" by the Grade Eights. The King and the Page and the old Man, and a chorus all on stage. No fake snow this year, just the same costumes. We didn't do a thing; I mean our class. Just got on the stage and sang a carol.

Mama says no Christmas this year. Does that mean no presents and no tree and no nothing? Almost. We can still go to Akiyama's and pick out whatever we wanted in their toy department, but that's it. No other presents. No turkey. Just us. And nowhere to go.

Wednesday, December 31, 1941 - The last day of the year! Went to the bath house early; told by Mama to get the year cleaned off but good. It's the custom to clean the house and pay off debts and all that. The least we could do is to clean our bodies. Went with Shoji. We have always gone to the bath behind the Sisters' Cafe. Nobody else was there. Just us. We soaked in the green and smelly herb bath for a change. After the bath we hung around at the back of the cafe and watched Chiyo jitterbugging with some guy. Actually it was late afternoon, before supper-time. Glenn Miller's "In the Mood" on the jukebox. We edged in and watched the record spinning around and glanced around at the jitter-buggers. The guy had on draped pants with a watch chain. "Mister whatcha call it, whatcha doing tonight...." Chiyo's long hair dancing. She looked at us and said, "Shake it up, boys."

Later I take out the school atlas and show Shoji a map of the world. Japan is a string of wiggly islands off the continent of Asia. America is big and Canada is bigger and the whole world is the biggest! I know that, Shoji says. He's eight years old. We thought we might sit the year out but

Mama

he falls asleep; I go into the kitchen and watch Papa make chicken teriyaki. He does it every New Year's Eve. He hums his song which he does every time he's doing something like this, cooking and basting chicken, or cooking up salmon eggs for fish bait, adding just the right amount of sugar, for colour, he says.

Mama prepares the Butsudan: she puts out dishes of oranges and mochi in front of the homemade wooden shrine which houses an image of Amida Buddha on a small brocaded scroll. The small doors of the shrine are open to receive them, and in a small brass urn incense is smoking. There is a little brass bell on a cushion, and to the side of it a small framed grey photograph of an old woman, Mama's mother, we understand. Obā-san, grandmother. Mama with prayer beads around her clasped hands bows in silence. Tomorrow she will ask us to stand with her in front of the shrine as she lights the incense again, and bow. But here to this home made shrine, the Butsudan, which Mama calls Hotoke-san, some times, and more often, Man-Man-san, she would bid one of us to take a small offering of rice each day. It would be the first scoop from the rice pot and it would be mounted in a small egg cup-like chawan. An every day ritual.

The year is ending. It was the Year of the Snake. I was born in the Year of the Snake and we have come the full cycle of twelve years. Tomorrow, a new year, and it will be the Year of Horse. Attributes of the snake: intuitive, philosophical, imaginative, and frequently physically beautiful; of the horse: rash, glib, entertaining, and a perfectionist. All from mama: who opens her remarks with: "*Yu to yaroka?* Shall I tell you? What would you like to know?"

Thursday, January 1, 1942 - *O-shogatsu*. New Year's Day. But nothing like the other years. No visitors, and almost no food. I mean special Japanese food. We did have some mochi and o-zoni, that's sticky rice cake and the special soup, and last night Papa did make his specialty, chicken teriyaki, and Mama did make nishime, the shogatsu dish that has all the virtues of good life symbolized by a vegetable or a foodstuff like rolled seaweed for good fortune and carrots for long life and sweet potato for good thoughts, and what all else… and that's it. Plus, *chikrashizushi*. And Mr. Akiyama did come by and give us each a silver dollar coin as he has always done on New Year's Day. But that was all. In the end I asked Mama, why? and she said it's because of the war. Mama says New Year's Day is a day for making resolutions for the coming year and thinking about the future. *Kakugo wo suru*, she says, brace yourself for the future.

Yesterday, I finished reading about Huw in his Welsh mining valley and felt really sad that he had to leave his family and home at the end. Storybooks come to an end, just like the movies. But I think about Huw, along and friendless, seeking another life outside his valley in the big wide world. How green was my valley. He can't go to Patagonia like the lovesick Reverend and be a missionary. But there must be somewhere else for him. Maybe he will join the merchant marine and sail the world many times over. What about me?

The Miyasakis call and I talk to Freddie. Not much happening there either. Everything is so quiet. We hadn't seen each other all of last month. Not since that Sunday. We agree to meet up sometime soon. Maybe the Saturday next. Go to a movie or something. Okay? What are you doing? We're all just playing Monopoly, he says, and Richard's got all the best, Park Avenue and Boardwalk. Good bye.

Our phone is in the shop on the near end wall to the living area. I have to stand on a box to get to speak into the mouthpiece and hold the hearing handle to my ear. Our number is Highland 456. You can adjust the mouthpiece up or down; and there are two bells at the top of the wooden box. You think you can see it ring. Mama stands on tip toes when she's at the telephone even though she doesn't have to.

Miyo tells me today that the best birthday party that she went to last year was at Yae Kitamura's. First of all, it was all girls; like Grace Kanda, all school friends. There were eight of them at the party and they had sworn a secret oath to be friends forever. What did you actually do, I ask, but Miyo doesn't answer. It's a secret, she says. But the funniest thing about the party for her was that while the sukiyaki was being cooked and served, Yae was feeding all the green onions, which she doesn't like, to her cat under the table. Sukiyaki, I said, that's fancy. What's sukiyaki?

Afterwards in the evening Rinzo came and we had manju and cakes and fruits as the old family albums were pulled out and the pictures gone over one by one. Rinzo thinks Japan will win in the end because the Pacific Ocean is just such a huge ocean and America will not be able to transport all the things necessary to wage war across such great distances. He went on about this point. That came about when Mama remarked that when she came over in 1928 it took 16 days to cross the Pacific. Papa came home from somewhere and sat at the table and smoked his cigarettes. He had on his dark suit and his spats, and of course when he was outside he always wore his dark fedora. At the table he didn't say very much, and then he brought out a deck of cards and we all played black jack, all except Mama.

Shin-nen omedeto. Greetings for the New Year.

Friday, January 2, 1942 - I don't know what I can say about today. I haven't made any resolutions for 1942. Maybe it should simply be that I'll keep writing this diary. Resolved! Saw Mits Tanaka at the Powell Street Drug Store. He gave me a sly look. I was going to buy a copy of Life Magazine. Mits scooted off when Mr. Shaw came around the front from behind the counter. Mits's family has the tofu shop couple of houses down from us. His brother Bill's the one who got that splinter in his eye. They all smell of the oily aburage, from the deep frying of the tofu to make age (Miyo thinks they all stink, but I kind of like that smell) and all the grown ups in that family who work in making the tofu have arms and hands that are red and blotchy. Bill says that's 'cause they are always in cold, cold water. The cold water is a constant in the wooden tubs where the tofu is made and get shaped. Mama says that the Tanaka's tofu is the best, but that the best aburage is at the Wakaybayashis, four houses further down. These shops are actually at the rear of the buildings, I mean the business doors are located in the alleyways.

Mits is known as the *itazura*, the *yancha* the mischief maker. Some of his stunts are well known. In my classes, especially at the Japanese school, he's pretty wild at times. When Sensei isn't looking he would signal that he's putting wads of gum on Shogo Kobayashi's seat as Shogo standing smartly gives a reading from the text, and the class would just bust out laughing. And then Shogo would sit down... Or during test times, he would pass out erasers with numbers on them to girls who would have to return them to him with the correct answers on them. The numbers related to the required correct character letters in the numbered boxes. And the giggling girls usually obliged. Mits has a way, I guess.

So Mits was at the Drug Store just looking it over. He's known to have a pretty fast pair of hands. He puts on an empty look, and... He had that look at the Sister's Cafe once when I was there and he was mooning over at the candy counter. Just then Eddie Baker, Flo's English boy friend, sauntered in and Mits took off. Eddie looks just like Fred Astaire, thin and wiry and coiled like a steel spring. He's an ex-boxer, so we've been told by Chiyo, but a very nice man, and he's from London, England. Wow, we said.

Monday, January 5, 1942 - "You're a sap, Mr. Jap," is hanging it on the Hit Parade and Tak is whistling it. He said today that people in Vancouver are still very upset because of the fall of Hong Kong to the Japanese on Christmas Day. There were a lot of Canadian soldiers who had just gone over there last November, and the survivors are now prisoners-of-war of the sneaky Japs. It's bad for us 'cause we're Japanese, no matter if we were born here. And another thing Tak said: Akiyama-sensei was one of those picked up by the Mounties immediately after Pearl Harbor and taken to the COR Immigration Building at Pier "C." Is he a spy? Wow, Hackenbush, a spy. "Never mind," Tak says, they think we're all spies. Chances are we'll be locked up.

All this after the school as I hung about the shop. Business is really falling off. All the fishing boats were brought in and locked up and there's nothing happening. Tak is taking an inventory. I help with stock talking, counting off the number of sheet metals in their various gauges, and boxes of bolts and screws and rivets and washers by the sizes and grades. No customer, nobody comes, except Frank Hod from next door. Sometimes he's called Hiroshi, mostly by his family, with us he's Frank. I guess we're all doing the same he says, taking stock. They run a dry goods grocery and have a big operation in the Fraser Valley with the strawberry farmers for which they have a special customers' man running about in a black Ford delivery van. His name is Mr. Uchikata and he's your prototype Jap, Tak would say. Horn rimmed glasses, buck teeth and all. Just passing the time, Frank says, flapping his arms and dancing about. He goes to King Edward High School, in Grade Nine. He wants to get into commerce when and if he goes to the university, UBC. In my life time, I'm out to make lots of money, he says throwing his hip out. Tak who really wants to get into Vancouver Technical High School full time and get a proper trade certificate for something like roofing and ventilation, doesn't say anything about Frank's wishes. Frank dances off.

Kilby dropped by, Bill Kilby, looking for Papa. Kilby calls him "Sam." Kilby is a bright looking guy and he's been in and out and around the shop for sometime now, but this is the first time since early last December. He has a soft voice and speaks kind of slowly. He feels good with us because he's always all smiles and ever cheerful, and today's no exception. And Tak likes him, too. I guess he's a few years older than Tak, maybe more.

He notes our stock taking and grunts after the no news of slow business, uses the phone and then leaves. Bill's been working on some deal about sawdust burners and has business arrangements with Papa who will make the sawdust hoppers. And these hoppers are made not from just your plain galvanized tin, no sir, these hoppers are made from sheets of stainless steel and are nickel plated. Papa and Tak have a made a number of them already. Both of them had become good acetylene welders to boot. So, according to Tak, all this is just in the making towards a really good business expansion some time soon, and that's one of the reasons why he's going to Vancouver Tech night school to learn more about electroplating and special welding and stuff. Are schools the only places to learn about things? How did Papa learn this business, and what am I myself learning at school?

Well, again at school we had the Air Raid Precautions drills: what to do in case of air raids and incendiary bombs are dropped. We had buckets of sand and shovels and were shown what to do, as if we didn't know already, by a special ARP warden, and old silver haired man who took his duty very seriously. Nobody dared to snicker. I recall having a great time the last occasion when we had these drills. That was a year or more ago when we all learned about the Battle of Britain and about civilian defence, and about the RAF and the Spitfire fighters: "Never before in the field of human conflict has so much been owed by so many to so few." Now, of course in the evenings the blackouts are in full force and we have blankets and curtains draped over the windows. You'd think we're learning to be really at war.

Thursday, January 15, 1942 - In mid afternoon Papa and some of the neighbourhood men had all gone to report to the Mounties' office, for which they hire Mr. Kitamura's Nabata Taxi. This reporting business is a once a month affair. But this time, there is some serious news: Many of the nationals, men like Papa who are Japan-born, are to be sent out to some kind of a camp, a work camp out in the wilds. I get all this from Tak after school. It's serious stuff, he says. This is going to become a "protected area" for 100 miles inland up and down the Coast, and no aliens are going to be permitted to stay in it. Aliens? Your father is an alien, he's a Japanese national, born in Japan. We're not aliens because we're Canadians, born in Canada. Does that mean in the war we're on the side of the Allies and Papa's with Japan and the Nazis? You got me there, Tak says, we can't join the army and fight for this country because we're Japs. But aren't they winning? It looks like it for now, but who knows for sure! Papa came back quietly and said he's off to talk with his friends at Sumiyoshi, his hangout on the next block down.

Tak is making what he thinks is the last of the stove pipes. I watch him go through a familiar routine: first, the two opposite edges of 22-gauge sheets of tin about two feet square are bent over nearly flat about a quarter of an inch or so by the sheet bender, operated by hand, and second, the sheet is rolled in through a set of rollers so that it comes out round and the edges join together in a clasp, and third, the clasped edges are rolled and bevelled in this funniest contraption of a hand machine (in war games it is a machine gun with the cranking handle like a Gatling gun), and then, fourth, the pipe, for it is already that, is slid through onto a steel rail, about six feet long and which is anchored onto a table (imagine how big and heavy these work tables are to support these heavy hand machine and this rail), and the clasped edges lightly hammered with a wooden mallet and a small rivet hammered in at the end that will be crimped on the crimping machine and which when joined up with another pipe will be the end that will slide into the other: and, finally, on the same end, a collar of double rolls from the same crimping machine but as a separate operation. And there you have it: stove pipes, our stock in trade. We join them up in lengths of threes and hoist them up to the struts over the work tables for storage keeping. All the machines are hand cranked and operated, with handles for right handers only. Tak says that's why when you exercise you have to favour your left arm so that it's getting its share of muscle building.

Tak has instructed me in all the phases so well that I can perform all of the functions and make saleable tin stove pipes. Then, too, I am a very good helper for him when he does the riveting of the water tank. I hold the heavy steel bar that cushions the hammer blows that flatten the rivets. He can do them on his own, but if I help him it's easier for him. So I'm useful in the shop. I can also look after the soldering irons and clean the heated irons in acid. They're called irons but they're actually made of copper.

So that's what we did this afternoon, after school. And at school today, there was a new face in the class, a Japanese guy, Hatsuo Uchida, from a place called Ocean Falls. Ocean Falls, sounds so much better than Niagara Falls. I asked Hats (that's what he said I should call him, 'Hats,') about the name "Ocean Falls", and he said it's 'cause the ocean water really falls like a waterfall at one point, depending on the tide though. He wanted to tell me more: that Ocean Falls is where they make paper from pulp wood, and about the fact that his father, an accountant at the paper mill had been laid off, figure it's 'cause of the war, and that's why they just came here, to Vancouver, him and his father and mother and a much younger kid brother. You never know what's going to happen, he shrugged. He has the curliest hair of anybody, but ask him a simple question and you get a history and a half, I thought.

Night time, and you can't go out. There's no more basketball games. I sit out in the shop and read The Shadow. Dime magazines. Lamont Cranston, the rich playboy by day, the clever crime fighter at night. Heh, heh, heh, only the Shadow knows! I sit out in the shop cause Miyo's practising the piano. The piano, the most expensive piece of furniture in our place.

Cost four hundred dollars. Nordheimer. Made in Toronto, it says: said to be the most modern of designs. And it came into the house less than a year ago. Upstairs, Naomi has one too, and I guess it's because of her and her mother that Miyo started taking piano lessons with Miss Mary Naka about two years go. This Miss Naka is a real lady, Miyo says, and she has the most elegant fingers, long and absolutely straight with no bony knuckles. And she's tall and slim and her hair is always elegantly coifed. Coifed? Yes, set, she says. They even had their picture taken together at the Columbia Studio, and she is in evening clothes, wearing a long dress with puffy sleeves, and her hair all swept up! It's quiet now and I am going to fall asleep.

Thursday, January 15, 1942 - Supper time was strange. Normally, Papa would eat quickly and move away from the table and smoke a cigarette in the other room (we eat in the kitchen at a round table), but tonight he sort of just sat in his chair. Then, too, he didn't eat with his usual gusto with lots of noise especially with the noodles in chicken broth we had. He's not a talkative person anyway, and he's not our disciplinarian. Mama does all that, correcting us, prompting us, giving us the morals on this or that, the good and the bad, even about standing straight and still. With Papa you had the feeling that if he explodes, that's it. And so you did whatever he asked, quickly and correctly. And there's a kind of routine with him. Tonight there's him just sitting there after the meal. And Mama's kind of quiet, too. Not that she's chatty herself. When there's food to dish up and as they say, *susumeru,* push forward, she would do that as a mater of course and urge you to eat some more. There's lots of food tonight, but she's not pushing it out like. Besides the noodles we had tempura too. Kind of special. Maybe something's cooking.

Saturday, January 17, 1942 - This evening out in the dark on the far side of Powell Grounds, under the big chestnut trees a bunch of guys were flashing about with luminous yo-yos, but I was struck by one guy who was gawking at me but gnawing away at a bony end of a pork chop. Where did he get this? Is that his supper? He was chewing steadily away and enjoying it so much I couldn't keep my eyes off him. Mama doesn't give us pork like that at her table, and we never have roast pork. Roast pork! At the Amemori's next door you can smell and see the pork cooking, and they eat it hot greasy and with lots of shoyu, and I guess Mrs. Amemori used to be a cook in a fishing camp or a logging camp, they have these huge cooking pots, and whenever the rice gets burned at the bottom, Haru-chan, the younger daughter, would make rice balls of it and give us burnt nigiri, burnt rice balls, black and white, with salt. And we eat them and like them, too.

Scotty's foot is all right more or less, he still limps about, but Rinzo has not found any work ever since Pearl Harbor Day when The Tairiku, the Japanese newspaper, was closed down. The way he rubs his jaws and crinkles his eyes.

There are three of them: Rinzo, Eizo (Scotty) and Kazuo. Of the three Scotty looks and acts the most like a *hakujin*[4]. He dresses sharper and smarter, with an ascot 'round his neck, a sports jacket, and with his wavy hair, and he's better looking. Rinzo and Kazuo, you'd call them Japan-boys. Straight, shortish hair, in Rinzo's case parted on the side, and very close at the back and the nape, and Kaz with short brush cut and gawky teeth and thin. There are two older sisters, Haru-chan and Yoshiye, and they are no great lookers either, not like Mary and Nancy behind us. The Amemoris. Their place is always kind of dark and smoky, and there's always a lot of roomers and boarders, and they have this huge round table around which everyone sits and eat, and you can see all this from the outside through their open door. And I guess you notice all this because

---

4   Literally, a 'white person', a Caucasian

the one and only bright light is right over the table and it has this great big green tin shade, like in a gambling den, and the rest of the place seems to be in semi-darkness. And they have their own bathhouse at the back, and Miyo and Sumi and Mama have been over to that bath a number of times. I've never been asked. I don't think Papa has been asked either. I had a look at it last summer when I helped them string up the antennae for their short-wave radio. It's a wooden tub, big enough for two people to soak fully right inside it.

And then in front of the Amemoris, fronting on to the street, live the Wakabayashis; and there's Terumi, she's in Grade Eight, and her much younger brother, Yoshikazu. Her father runs a small one truck transport business called Maruchu Transport. It has a nice sign: on a field of yellow, in black, a circle, for the "maru" which means "circle," and inside of that the character for "chu" which means "inside." Maru-chu. So, Mr. Wakabayashi is known as "Maru-chu-san," and everybody calls him that. He wears a leather apron when he's working, driving and hauling.

Sunday, January 24, 1942 - Today Miyo and I went to visit our cousins in Steveston. We left the house in midmorning, and at the B.C. Electric Railway terminus behind Beacon Theatre on Hastings Street, we caught the trolley car for Steveston.

It's a rambling trip on a tooneyville car, just like in the comics. We pass Lansdowne Park and Brighouse Park, racing tracks for thoroughbreds, where Papa once took me along and Mama was angry that he did: she said it to his face when we got back. The trolley crosses over onto Sea Island, and then Lulu Island and finally comes to a full stop right in front of the Steveston Japanese Language School, and then turns around for the return trip. Steveston.

Uncle Jiro, Papa's twin brother but not identical, owns the Home Oil gas station scow out in the middle of the river at Steveston. Cousin

George who's two years older than me would take us out there in the rowboat with an outboard motor, and I would be so envious and yet so thrilled by his performance. He did it with such a flourish! Once we were seated, he would kick the motor into action and give it lots of gas, and with the roar and a sharp thrust of the steering handle he would twist turn the boat out into the river and steer it straight for the scow, all the while standing. I would be like laughing and crying. Not any more. No more fishing, no more scow, no more boats. We didn't go near the river at all today.

Aunty speaks English just like us and she's not even a Nisei. She's a member of the United Church and a regular church goer. She wears black-rimmed glasses and looks like a school marm. She bakes wonderful pies and cakes, and in her kitchen we eat things we never see at home. Simple things like corn on the cob and coffee from a percolator, and roast beef with terrific gravies! And potato salads. And in season, cherry pies. There are two cherry trees at the side of the house, and what fun we would have picking them every year. Big Byng cherries. And she makes jams and pickles. We call her Aunty, not Oba-san.

Aunty and Uncle Jiro were the *baishakunin*, or the go between, for Fu-chan when she got married last year. Fu-chan is Mr. Akiyama's eldest daughter and she is Mama's dear friend. Our youngest, Sumi, was one of the flower girls at the wedding. Fu-chan married a Steveston man, but he's not a fisherman. Mr. Tamaki is a suit-wearing businessman. We did not see them.

Miyo went off with Yuri, our cousin. Now the curious thing about Yuri or Lily is that we know she's adopted but we wonder if she knows. We never asked. Anyway, we call her Lily, and the funny thing is Aunty does too. Yuri means Lily. After a lunch of chicken soup and sandwiches, George and Ian, my other cousin and the youngest of us three, went off and loped about the school yard across the road. I showed off my wrist watch. George hauled out his pocket watch and we compared times. He said a pocket watch is safer, meaning you can't break it so easily.

Later we went down Moncton Street, Steveston's one and only, and hung about the poolroom. A lot of men were there jabbering away. I could never understand what a guy from Steveston is saying, in Japanese or in English. But one young guy at the pool hall was really angry as he faced a group in the hall. He was saying we had the best goddamn year last year, and me, I finally got a boat of my own, and I know that this year is going to be even better, and I had plans to laid out to buy more net, and what the hell they take our boat and now they say they're going to be sold, but the boat's all swamped up. No goddamn good for anybody. What the hell's going on, he demanded to know. Nobody had any answer. The click-click playing on the pool tables resumed. Now everybody's out of work. There's no fishing, and of course no work in the canneries. And no gas station scows. At the Kuba's General Store, a big place handling most anything that can be sold, Kuba-san, his wife and others, were packing stuff away. They are Aunty's kinfolks. Miyo was there with Lily, and they had given her dress material for Mama, and candies and cakes for us to take home.

It started to rain as the trolley crossed over the tram bridge at Sea Island and the clouds hung low over Grouse Mountain. Rumbling above False Creek we are nearly at the terminus and home: below, it is a mess of sawmills, lumber yards and sawdust bins; in the waters, log rafts and scows with more lumber and garbage and junk and even shack-houses.

Back home I try out the Japanese dialect that they speak in Steveston saying: "*onsha, waisha,* and *gaina,*" (meaning: you, me and gee whiz!) with every other phrase. Nobody thinks its particularly funny. Oh, well. After a trip to Steveston I always put on that talk and that swagger of the fishermen. Mama asks after Aunty and everybody and Fu-chan, and Miyo fills her in. Except Fu-chan because we didn't see her. It was nice to spend the day in Steveston with George and Ian and Lily and Aunty and Uncle Jiro.

Friday, January 30, 1942 - After school went with Hats to his place. They have a couple of rooms in this rooming house called Sun Rooms and that's next to the Fuji Chop Suey House, and downstairs is the Pool Hall. And all this is on 300 block Powell Street, across from Taishodo, the Japanese non-prescription drugs and gift store. Hats' mother was there and she is nice: she split us a bottle of Orange Crush into two small glasses. We took that in one gulp and then went around to look the place over. I've never been around rooming houses like this before. We walked over to the back and climbed up and down and looked over Powell Street below. It wasn't that high, you couldn't see the harbour clearly, but the landmarks were there, the mountains, the Lions, and the Marine Building, and the people down below weren't exactly ant-size.

The cooking from the chop suey houses smelt really good. After a while we came down and hug about the pool room. Peanuts was there, just practising. He was squinting through his cigarette smoke and making the shots. I couldn't tell a good set up from a bad one, not like Hats, but from the sharp click of the one ball hitting another and the solid sound that ball made when it hit the back end of the pocket as it was knocked in, said something about how Peanuts was playing. But then other players made those sounds too. But I knew from Tak that Peanuts is a pool shark so I watched him, until a bossy guy dressed in a tight suit and waving a toothpick told us, sharply, in Japanese to beat it: "*Oi! kozo! kaere!*" (Hey, kid! Go home!) Peanuts looked up and waved good-bye. I said, see ya, Hats, and went home.

Friday, February 6, 1942 - At school someone said that all the Japanese would be sent out of town. I ask Hats who said that, and he says he heard that too. It's called rumour. My Dad said that about rumours, he said.

He calls his father, "Dad." I remark on that to him, and he says at home he calls him "To-chan," and mother, "Kaa-chan."

In the art class I'm working on a poster for a cleanup campaign and I have a picture of a garbage can made out of tin, naturally, with the open lid as the mouth and the lid as the head with bug eyes and a big nose, with skinny arms from the handles stuffing cans and newspapers into the mouth, and with a banner headline: "Stuff your garbage can!" The garbage can is modelled after one of our own makes. Rose looks over her huge glasses and says: Heedeeo, that's good! and I am warm and tingly with her smile. But our resident genius with the pencil and paint and crayon and brush is Noboru Matsuda, or Gabby. He could draw Mickey Mouse better than Disney himself. When he writes he dots his "i's" with a small circle. Someone said that shows artistic talent, and for awhile we all dotted our "i's" like that.

The yo-yo sales-guy was out in the yard this morning before the opening bell. My favourite trick of his is the last one when he spins the yo-yo and he loosens the string from his finger and then he flings the yo-yo into the air and catches it with the string all wound up. Better than his biggest a trip-around-the-world! Back at home and in the shop you'd think the shop is about to take a trip or something. After the stock taking, things are getting squared away, and now some machines are being crated. Or rather, wooden crates are being made. Papa and Tak-chan are working on some plan, I guess. I'm in the way and not much of a help.

Across the street on the fringes of the Ground, Kaz and some guys are getting around for a game of marbles. I pick up my bag and go and join them. Kaz is the youngest Amemori and a year or more older than me. He runs all the games he's going to play which means you have to play by his rules, more or less. Which means he's the judge of close calls. Hunching over the game are Roy Miyasaki and his brother Herb, they're Freddie's cousins, and their father is Harry Miyasaki and he has this Harry's Cleaners on Hastings Street. And there's Junji Kinoshita, a snotty, petty guy. And another Kinoshita but not relation, Yoshimi. And Mits. I say, not bad! to Mits as he scores a nice round and wins three marbles. He laughs. So, it's the Cordova Street guys against us; Kaz, and Mits and me.

Marbles. A circle is drawn on the ground with a stick, with the size of the circle depending on the number of players; in the middle a smaller tight circle is drawn in to which each player puts in a marble or two, the ante. The order of shooting is decided by each player tossing or shooting his shooter from a prescribed distance to the line of the circle. Closet one gets to shoot first and so on. You shoot your shooter with your hands back side down, with all your four big knuckles touching the ground (very important). The shooter is placed between the first knuckles of the thumb and the curved over forefinger. The middle finger holds the thumb down, and the other two fingers curve in sympathy and style. You shoot by flicking the thumb out. You can shoot with either hand, and after awhile your knuckles would get red and sore and bleeding. A seasoned marble player has real scabby knuckles. Some players use pads but they are considered sissies. Shooting from the rim of the circle into the cluster of marbles at the centre, the idea is to knock one of them cleanly out of the circle (it's yours then) and to keep your shooter inside the circle. As long as it's in, you can keep shooting, moving directly into the circle to do so. The object of the game is to knock out as many marbles as you can. To make the game more interesting the players may throw in more than one or two marbles into the pot. There are other ways, like you can play in squares, or rectangles, or you can play with steel balls in various sizes (from garages.) It's important to have a distinctive shooter so that every player could recognize the marble as yours. Cat's eyes or streaky or clear or murky colours or candy stripes and so on.

There are other games we play out on the Grounds. Like hit-the-stick.

Okay, you have two pieces of sticks. One is less than half the length of the other, and they're both about half an inch thick. A small sloping hole is dug into the ground and the short one is propped into it with the end sticking out. Now the longer stick is taken in hand and you hit the short one on its end and send it up in the air, and you try to hit it once, twice, thrice.... with a final big smash to send it hurtling away. Given the number of times you were able to tap it, you pace and count the distance back to the hold with the short stick, doubling or tripling or quadrupling the count, and the winner is one who scores the most in a certain number of tries. In hit-the-stick, Kaz is the best, in fact he always seems to with no matter what the game! Me, I don't do well at any of them, but I like to join and play when I can, and when they let me. The game of marbles. We play on into the dusk. Shoji runs over and comes to call me home. Supper-time. What, is it that kind of time? Kaz asks, and the game breaks up. I didn't do too bad, won about eight marbles. Mits, too. See, ya, he says, and stuffs his marbles into his pockets and runs off, the laces of his running shoes all undone. Tie your laces, I yell. He looks down and shrugs and hops over the street car tracks. Mits.

Saturday, February 14, 1942 - Uncle Jiro and Cousin George come up from Steveston, Yuri/Lily too. Cousin George and Uncle Jiro and Papa and me, we all go to Fuji Chop Suey House for lunch, Nanking soba, Chinese noodles. Papa gives us the money to go to see a double bill at the Beacon Theatre. Dead-end Kids in "Little Tough Guys" and Dick Foran in "Mob Town," two gangster type films. Lep Gorcey talking tough and slapping other Kids about. We walk quickly back to Powell Street and George treats me to that good old Boston Cream pie at the Empress Cafe. Then we rejoin Uncle Jiro and Yuri and they drive off back to Steveston.

Later, Miyo tells me that Lili went to see her real sister, or at least what Miyo thinks is her real sister. Did you know, she says, that it's that girl who lives with the Uchida family, Dr. Uchida? They're sisters! And you know what? They look alike! "What do you mean? Did you take her there?"

"Yes," she says, "Uncle Jiro said 'Yuri is to go see this girl', gosh, she must be about eighteen, and her name is Diane. He said I should take Yuri-chan and ask for the doctor, and she will have a little visit over there. So I did that."

"Didn't you stay?"

"No, I just walked up that stairway taking Lily by the hand, and this girl, Diane, she was waiting for her at the top. I'd seen her before. I think she goes to a high school. Poor Lily. She didn't say anything after. She's so quiet. Gee, they sure look alike." Miyo looks about thoughtfully, softly: did you know, she says, "That Taka-chan gave me the name Margaret?" After that Princess, Margaret Rose? Remember the Coronation?

Tuesday, February 17, 1942 - Papa got his orders to go to road camp. I guess he was expecting it. He was looking relieved. As if he wasn't in suspense about it anymore. Now it's clear what's going to happen, to him anyways. It will be early in March he says. He's talking to Tak. They want all the Japan-born, 18 to 45 years old, to be out of Vancouver. You see, he says, it's the age for active military service. I think about his brother, Rokuro who's an infantryman in the Japanese Army; there's that photo of him holding the Japanese flag wide open and on it are the signatures of well-wishers spreading out like the rays of the sun. And such a look on that uncle whom I've never met. A face of resolution.

This order then, is it like that, a military call up for Papa? I ask Tak later. Not really, he's not going to war, your Pop and all the Isseis he says, and I don't know what road camp means either, but I guess they're going to work on roads and live in camps. In the mountains, the Rockies, somewhere. Why? I want to know. Well, Tak says, they want to get ride of the Japanese in Vancouver and places like that. Listen, Spike, I don't know, they just don't like us here. We're Japs. But then Mama says later that Papa is going because then others will not have to go. He's going for our sake. I don't understand it at all.

Monday, February 23, 1942 - Our radio, at the suggestion of Mr. Oya, is to be entrusted to him for safekeeping. It will be put in the care of Mrs. Booth, a person who works for the newly organized Security Commission which is to look after the Japanese. Mr. Oya should know about these things, agrees Mama. She also takes down the framed photograph of that invincible Japanese battle cruiser on which her brother serves. Not only does she take it down, she destroys it, burns it up. Why do you do that, I ask her. Because, she says, some things have to be done. Rinzo comes over to say that we can listen to their radio if we want to: it's in Scotty's room at the back. It's a powerful short wave radio, the antennae had been put up last summer, cleverly strung along the edge of the building next to them, the Maruno's big fish market, and so not visible. Rinzo waits for the Japanese news: it is preceded by the Japanese naval anthem, "Gunkan March" (The Battleship March). We all know this from the Japanese school days. It's one of our favourite marching songs. And then the news. Rinzo gives a running commentary: Philippines and the battle of Coral Sea, the victories in New Guinea. And a statement about the Imperial destiny of Japan. Meanwhile, it is announced that here in Vancouver we can expect a curfew, a dawn to dusk curfew in a few days. Just for us.

Saturday, February 28, 1942 - Dawn to dusk curfew! Seven thirty, and we hang about the front of the shop as the curfew time comes. Out on the grounds Mits is running around yelling his head off: "curfew time, curfew time!" His brother Bill chases him home. Papa sneaks off to Sumiyoshi, he says to Mama. We stare after him, fearful for him: Miyo says, gee willikers!

Later we see a group of men running across the grounds, and then a mounted policeman spots them and gives chase. Across on Cordova street, the men make it through to a narrow passageway between two houses. Too wide for the horse. We give a cheer and pop back into the shop. We are Scotty, Kaz, Miyo, Shoji, Terumi and me. After the others go, I sit out on the counter and watch the night. Nothing else happens. But Papa? But Papa. A very quiet man. Compared to say Uncle Jiro, his twin, or to Mr. Miyasaki. Now these two are not blabber mouths or anything like that but they are simply loquacious compared to Papa. That's from Tak, that word, like sarcastic, or, another good, pugnacious. Papa says you learn by watching, and he shows you, but he doesn't tell you or demonstrate. You're supposed to pick it up. Just like that. He's got strong arms and a wash board belly, and he's not good for drinking anything alcoholic. His favourite food however is fermented tofu, a Chinese delicacy. Fermented, that's alcoholic, no? It stinks like hell. He gets it in Chinatown. And he simply puts it away at nearly every meal time, on hot rice. We know he's got to go soon but we don't know anything. Where, or how long, and why? We know Uncle Jiro is going too, at the same time, that's understood. And Oji-san's got a new place for Aunty and George and Ian and Yuri, a farm across the Fraser at New Westminster. And while he's gone, they're supposed to sit out the war on this farm. Uncle Jiro has plans, or dreams or something.

Papa doesn't say anything or do anything. No, that's not true. He's machines and things will be stored away in a warehouse, and the stock will be sold, and Tak and Bill Kilby will look after all the little things. That's what Tak said. Yes, and everything's going to be looked after and everything's going to be all right.

Tuesday, March 3, 1942 - The date is set for Papa, it's March 10, a week today, and the road camp, a place called Red Pass, near Jasper. And Papa's got his new outfit: a pair of hobnailed boots, from Pierre Paris, the best bootmakers in town, says Tak. I know where it is, on Hastings Street, near Rex Theatre. And warm Siwash sweaters (all the fishermen have one), and breeches, and flannel shirts, like lumberjacks, and a fishing gear! A fly rod and reel! I tough them very carefully, and he joins up the rod and lets me flex it. And the reel, a gun metal one, flat and light, and the fly hooks and the tapered line, thin at the head and thick at the tail, so that when it is cast, the line will settle in on the water before the fly. And a light fold-up net. Gee willikers! Fly fishing! Well, we've never done that kind of fishing, but I've heard all about it from Roy, Freddie's cousin, and we've looked at some of the gear at Mc and Mc's. Gee, Papa, I say. There's good fishing in the Rockies, he says. Rainbow trout and brook trout and Dolly Varden. I shake my head in amazement. He takes the rod and the reel apart and puts them back into the carrying tube and case. Someday, he says, I'll show you how. What about you, I ask, do you know? And he says there's someone in their unit going to the road camp who's the real expert, and he's going to watch him. Nishihara-san, from Fairview, he's a steelhead fisherman, reels them in with four-ounce-test leaders. Wow, definitely no more still fishing for us.

Tuesday, March 10, 1942 - We were up early because Papa leaves today. But we have to go to school, so we said 'good bye, Papa,' and left for school. When we got back he wasn't there. Mama went down to the station and saw him off, she said, and Jiro-san was there too, and many friends of Papa; they were all going to the same camp. Mr. Sato and even Mr. Ito, Bobby Ito's father. So he's going to be all right, she said. He's with his friends, and *Nii-san* (Uncle Jiro) is there. Nii-san (big brother) because Jiro-san was born a few minutes before Papa, so Papa is Saburo, the third son, and Jiro number two son. Number one son had returned to Japan four years ago with his family. Never a direct letter from any of them to me, but I remember them: Nobuo, Eiji, Isamu and Kiyoshi. Mama used to say they were having a hard time because they didn't speak any Japanese, none at all. So Papa went. Gone fishing.

At school George Iwata from another Grade Seven class came up to me and said, my Pop's going to the same camp with your Pop. Is that right, I said. At school there are new faces, too. Kids from places outside Vancouver, like Hats. Oh yeah, and he said his Pop was going to be off to the road camp next week. Yellowhead Pass, he said. Red Pass, Roger's Pass, Yellowhead Pass... road camps. They're all around Jasper, he said. And new faces in the neighbourhood, too. Sam Sonoda from Woodfibre, he was sitting in the working chair of the barbershop of Mr. Yamagishi when I went for a *tokoya*, a hair cut. A heavy set guy, couple of years older, with a friendly face, he is saying to *tokoyasan*[5] that he quit school over a year ago, and had been working in the paper mill. Now, they're all here in Vancouver because they've all been fired, and there's nothing there and seems like there's nothing here too. From Woodfibre. Strange names. He's living with his father in the rooms up above the barbershop. Mrs. Yamagishi gives me the usual hard time with my haircut, or rather my head. She has always claimed that it's much too big for a kid and has charged adult rates for some time and she never fails to make comments about this whenever I go and today's no exception. I should tell her that Papa had to buy me an *otona* (adult) size hat last year at T. Maikawa but I suffer in silence to her jibes. Sam hangs around and laughs at all this.

So, today Papa went to the road camp. Mama got a telephone call from Mrs. Miyasaki. I answered when it rang in the evening and she asked after all of us and said that there was nothing to worry about and that I should come and visit Freddie, and then I got Mama to come to the phone. She was on the telephone a long time.

---

5 The barber

Monday, March 16, 1942 - A new girl, in the class today, from Woodfibre. Miss Bolton made a fuss for her, we all had to move one seat up because this new girl had to sit in the front of the second row. Her name is Christine, Christine Uno. When she was introduced some kids laughed at the name, and it's become a small joke, 'You know, Uno?' It should be said "uoono," not "yuno."

Then it came to the literature class and I had to stand up and give my recitation. I tremble with fear on these occasions and this time it is no exception. I find myself standing directly in front of Christine's desk and as I lift my eyes off the floor to begin I see her dazzling smile. The lines from Arthur Hugh Clough flow freely: "Say naught that the struggle availeth naught, that the struggle and the labour are in vain...." to the last one: "For look to the west, the land is bright." Floating to my seat I brush her desk, I swim in happiness. Walking home from school Mits catches up to me and wants to know about this new girl in my class. How does he know this? He's heard the joke and has seen her. (Mits is in the same grade as me but in Miss Johnson's class.) I tell him, she's from Woodfibre, and her full name is Christine Mitsuko Uno. Mitsuko! Just like his, he says. No, I says, If it were, yours would be Mitsuo, not Mitsuru. Close enough, he says, Mitsuru, Mitsuko. Christine, I says. Do you know where she lives, he asks. No, but I think its one of the rooming house/hotel on Hastings past Princess Avenue. Let's go and see her, he says, after supper. Well, we did, or tried to. We go by the alleyways along Hastings Street and find three rooming-house/hotels, choose one and try the front and the back doors. Closed. Out in the back there's a small yard with a shed, and we call out her name, No answer. A man, a hakujin, passing by and demands to know what we were doing, and where we lived, and all that. We quit after that and head for home. It's curfew, too.

I'll ask her tomorrow, Mits says. No, leave it to me. I will. And we went home.

Tuesday, March 17, 1942 - Well, I didn't have the nerve to ask, and Mits ran after her to ask after the school, and she wanted to know what for, and then said she can't have visitors and there's no place to play around her way, and well, good-bye. We think about that, Mits and I, for a while, and then we think that maybe we should take her to the Star Theatre and see a movie on Saturday. Well, we'll have to ask her, but maybe we should figure how to do it because neither of us has any money. I think of Mama, but it's not too good, with Papa away allowance time is over, and I'm not doing anything in the shop.

Did you know Mits says, that she has a sister, her name is Mieko. So what? Well, it'd be good if we take her too. She's in your sister's class, Mits says. You can look after her. Not me, you! I say, and we laugh.

But we worked it out on how we're going to get the money. We'll collect old bottles, first of all, down by the bushes of Railway Street and around the Canco "jungle," and sell them to the junk man on Alexander Street, you can get 2 or 3 cents a bottle, and Mits says he has a few tricks up his sleeve. We'll start this Saturday. Okay? I say. Mits punches me in the biceps and runs off jumping like a rabbit.

Saturday, March 21, 1942 - 80 cents, that's all we got from our bottles. We started out by going down to the Canco and then along the railway tracks to Gore Avenue, and backtracking up to Ballantyne Pier. We had my red metal wagon, a toy really, and we started out early. But that's all we made. 2 cents a bottle is all we got from Herman the German, the junk dealer on Alexander Street. Stinky whiskey bottles. Mits sniffs up a deep draught from each of the bottle he finds. We poke around the bushes and look about the small clearings with traces of camp fires, and kick about burnt out tin cans and cardboard cartons and boxes and newspapers and rubbish. Below us on the CPR tracks, a yard locomotive shunts back and forth looking for stray and empty boxcars. With only 80 cents in our pockets we have to do something. Mits says watch me. We are in the alleyway behind the Amano's, a miso factory place. In their backyard are empty tubs. Using a telephone pole to climb onto the fence, Mits pitches down two tubs from a pile. He instructs me to take them along to the front of the shop and sell them back to Mr. Amano. Loading them on the wagon I go to the front and ask for Mr. Amano. He comes out and says, ah, I know your father, what do you want. I point to the tubs, and say would you buy these? He comes out and inspects them and then walks over to the corner where he gives a shout. He's spotted Mits and knows what's up. I stand transfixed as he comes back to where I'm trembling.

You should not be with that *itazura*, that *tofuya no kozo*, he says, we've caught him before. Leave those tubs here, go home. Don't let me catch you doing silly things like this. I will speak to your mother. Drenched in shame I wheel the wagon homewards. Mits catches up to me. Come on, let's go spend our money. And we did that. We went to Star Theatre and saw "Perils of Nyoka," a serial and a Hopalong Cassidy picture with Gabby Hayes, and then we went and bought some comic books, Superman for me.

Monday, March 23, 1942 - Could hardly wait for today and for school to start. I was so relieved to know that Christine is all right and back at her desk in our class. What was I thinking of? Just looking at her makes me feel good, as if everything in the world is all right. Rose caught me following Christine with my eyes when she was at the blackboard. No smile, she just pursed her mouth tightly. After school I was following her home when Mits caught up to me. Not to be outdone I ran after her and we both caught up to her. She was with her sister. I said, Hi, and she said, Oh hi. I said, this is my friend, Mits. And she said, this is my sister, Mieko. And Mits said, can we come over to your place. And she said, I have to help my mother. And I said, can we see you on Saturday. And she said, maybe. Where do you live, Mits asked. And she pointed to the building. On the third floor, she said. We could all go to the Star, I said, on Saturday. Maybe, she said, good bye.

We ran all the way back to Powell Grounds. At the corner by the street car stop, there was a small group of young guys standing around, all strangers to our world, but all Japanese. One guy had a pork pie hat and his trousers were rolled up past the ankles, another had on an ascot, a small scarf knotted under his white shirt. They had a swank look, but countrified. There's a word in Japanese: *inaka mon*, meaning from the sticks. Roy Miyasaki, looking up from his marble game said, you know where those guys are from? They're from Hastings Park. Can you beat that? They're all from up the coast somewheres, like Skeena. Ever hear of Ucuelet? Hastings Park, yes, we've heard that some of the buildings have been taken over to house these people being moved to Vancouver from places up and down the coast. Hastings Park, the exhibition grounds and Happyland. A pause in the game: I heard that everybody in there got sick, Stomach ache, and the runs. Bad food. What do you expect? Lots of cow shit and horse shit. Everyone laughs. The streetcar comes and the group gets on. Back to Hastings Park. As they get on the street car they huddle at the back and look out over the open window. They don't look lost, only curious.

Saturday, March 28, 1942 - Today is a big day for Mama. She has arranged to have our family portrait taken, without Papa, at the Woodward's Department Store at Hastings and Granville. Woodward's because all the Japanese places are closed up. Woodward's! We don't like that place. We've always had been treated roughly by the sales people at this place. Especially us kids. But Haru-chan had made the appointment, and Mama says it's for *"kinen,"* a commemoration and a testament. Actually it was all right. The studio photographer was rather nice to us. A young man with sharp pointed chin and straight up hair, he talked about trolling for salmon in Horseshoe Bay last weekend. This after he got me to tell him that I liked to go fishing. And I guess we all laughed because he was telling us something we knew, fishing and Horseshoe Bay and all that, but I think he liked what he was doing and he liked us.

After that Mama took us back to Powell Street and we went to Sumiyoshi and had banana splits and sodas. Shimada's place is just about the last place that's open. Taji, the son, was behind the counter, serving and dishing out the sundaes. Mrs. Shimada came out and sat with Mama and chatted away. They talked about Papa and all their friends.

From left: Miyo, Hideo, Sumi, Mama and Shoji, taken at Woodward's Department Store.

Sunday, March 29, 1942 - As planned yesterday, went with Miyo to see our cousins again but this time out past New Westminister, across the Patullo Bridge to a place called Strawberry Hill. Uncle Jiro had bought this farm before he went the road camp to put his family in a safe place, is his thought. And today, Mama wanted us to go and see for ourselves where the place is and how it is and to tell her all about it. We went by bus, and got off at the right stop. Johnson's Road, Aunty had said, and we had gotten off at the right place, but turned the wrong way. So we found out half hour or so later by my watch when the apple orchard that was the key description of the place could not be found. We turned around and went back to where we started; back on the highway we crossed it, and found ourselves on the right road. By then, George and Ian were out looking for us, and Yuri, too, so the five of us marched happily to this farm.

It's a small vegetable farm with just about everything except cows and horses. There were chickens in the yard, and the cock strutted about. The big root cellar is our air raid shelter, said George. We laughed at that one. But the cellar is well stocked with potatoes, carrots, cabbages, onions, and preserves, and dried herbs. Aunty looked pleased. They could sit out this war right here. Uncle Jiro had it all figured out! George pointed to the south and said, look there's Tacoma Fuji. Low on the horizon was a cone shaped mountain. That's Mt. Hood, in the State of Washington, he said, see it's just like Fujiyama in Japan. Not too late in the afternoon, we started back, and when we got home and reported to Mama, she said: "*Anshin shita*, I'm relieved to hear all that." Are we going to live there, too, I ask. No, she says, we have no plans. We have to wait on the government to tell us what to do. We can't do anything on our own. We have to wait until Papa comes back, maybe sometime soon. Maybe.

Monday, March 30, 1942 - Wow! Walked Christine back to her place after school! How did it happen? I don't know. We were both late getting out of our class, finishing some work, I guess, and so when we got out we just started walking. Down Jackson and east along Hastings, with no thought. Actually I was telling her all about the visit to cousin George's and she was laughing a lot about the root cellar. And then she said it's so nice to be able to have a place like that in the country. Thinking about the book I'd read some time ago I said, yes, "Five Acres and Freedom." Your own farm and self-sufficiency. Did you see Charlie Chaplin in the "Modern Times?" No, she says, and I go prattling on about the tramp's dream about the idyllic country living: the tramp cranks the tail of the cow to get his fresh milk as the cow strolls conveniently by his doorway.

I tell her about the time Papa took me to see Chaplin's "The Great Dictator" at the new Plaza Theatre on Granville Street. It was a real big treat. First, the lunch at Melrose Cafe near the downtown CPR station (Papa had done some work in the kitchen, making a big new ventilation canopy), and then the movie. Can I treat you to a movie, I ask. My Aunty gave me a whole dollar, I blurt out. How about this Saturday? She says, yes, yes. I run home happy.

Saturday, April 4, 1942 - All week long I waited for today. To take Christine to the movies. And I did, and we went to the movies. And Mits, too. She and I are to met at the Rex Theatre to see "Dr. Jekyll and Mr. Hyde" starring Spencer Tracy, and when I get there ahead of time, Mits is there. Mits! He knew about it. I found out from her, he says. Don't worry, I can pay my way, he says. When she comes, she kind of surprised to see him too. What are you doing here, she asks. Mits just shrugs. We all go in. She sits between us. After the movie she says she's really sorry but she's got to go. Her mother isn't feeling well, and she left her with Mieko, and her father's not there, and all that. And all that.

I had planned on going to Ernie's or some place and have a soda or something. So I said meaningfully to Mits, see ya later, and I walk her to the street car stop and get on the car with her and walk her back to her place. I got that, at least. And we talked. She says sometimes soon, maybe as early as next week, they are going to have to move in to Hastings Park. We have to, she says. Her older brother has already been sent to a road camp in Ontario, a place called Schreiber, and they can't stay in this rooming house any longer. I'm going to miss Strathcona, she says, I really got to like it here. I could come and see you at Hastings Park, I says, it's not far. I've been there many times, every year there's the Exhibition, a real big fair time, and we used to have so much fun there. All those rides, Shoot-the-Chute, and the Giant Dipper, and candy cotton and hot dogs and caramel corn and french fries, and the fireworks.

Well, it's not going to be like that, is it? she asks. I guess not, I agree. Gee, I wonder what's going to happen to us all, she says. She looks up to see Mieko looking down at us, and gives her a wave, and gives me the sweetest smile and turns to go. I walk home along Cordova Street in the warm sunny late afternoon glow.

Sunday, April 5, 1942 - This afternoon after lunch I strapped on my roller skates and went down along the route I used to take to go to Stanley Park. First down Powell Street to Main and then down to the waterfront by the CNR Pier, and over to the dock for the North Van ferry, and along a short strip of a street, there a marine engineering works with the big store window framing a huge display case of a big model sailing ship, the Bluenose schooner, about four feet long, and ever so nicely done. A long lingering gaze, and then on to the CPR Station and then today below that the Immigration Building. Nearby the building but not too close to it, there's a small knot of Japanese guys looking up at the barred windows. On the third floor of this four floor structure, some heads can be seen, and hands waving out. They are the *ganbari-yas* I'm told, the holdouts who refuse to go to camps. Many of them were caught in The

Tairiku Building not more than two weeks ago. There are maybe a 100 of them inside this place. Some one says: watch it, it's going to come. A window frame is clear of the heads, the lower half of the window is open: through the bars something is thrown out. A piece of paper wrapped about piece of brick. When it lands it is quickly picked up, the paper smoothed out, and the contents read. It is a list of names. The knot of men move off and disappear. I look up at the faces in the windows and continue to wave to them.

I don't tell anyone of this. If Tak were about in the shop I would. But it's all dark and quiet there. What's happened to Tak anyway? We haven't heard anything from him, or at least I haven't. One night last week his girl friend, Penny came by. I mean she didn't come to the door but sort of called out, "Spike, spike," and I came out, and she wanted to know whether Tak was here with us. I said no, and she melted away. Just about curfew time, too.

And over at Horizon's, the dry-goods store next to us, Mr. Uchikata is on the lam, we've been told. He's supposed to have been on his way to the road camp but he didn't report to the station. Maybe he's held in that jail-like Immigration Building, too. Mild, Mr. Uchikata. At night in the alley ways, there's a lot of movement of people, men scurrying about from doorway to doorway, or going through the myriad of little passageways between houses and buildings along Powell Street. And often policemen on horsebacks clop-clop down the streets. And of course, there are the police cars, unmarked, cruising about. I don't know. But I think so.

Wednesday, April 8, 1942 - It's Hastings Park for Christine, next Monday. Miss Bolton is very sorry to hear about this and says so. She really got to like her, I guess. Others in the class, too. Dawn and Evelyn and Rose and Michi, they all became pals with Christine. We've had a couple of new faces, but she is the first to leave our class. We decide to have a little party on the last period of Friday. Everybody could bring a little something, cookies or a piece of cake. It will be for our first evacuee, Miss Bolton says. Evacuate, to withdraw; evacuation, a withdrawal; evacuee, a person withdrawn... Rather: evacuate, to take away; evacuee, a person taken away.

Saturday, April 11, 1942 - Yesterday's class party for Christine was a party! Gabby and Franklin Lee did a skit "An 'ole in th' Road" about two workmen who can't do anything right, Rose and fat Eva sang a song, "Mairzey Doats," and Christine herself with Miss Bolton at the piano sang "The White Cliffs of Dover" and we all were misty-eyed. "There'll be bluebirds over the white cliffs of Dover, tomorrow just you wait and see...."

She said she's going to a friend's place for the weekend, and then on Monday morning, Hastings Park. I hotly promise to come see her there. And today, bottle business with Mits continues, and we also went fishing for shiners off the old Hastings mill. We made fifty cents each from the bottles and 25 cents each from the bucket of shiners. The one and only Maruno's, the last place that will buy. We talk about Christine. For no good reason other than the fact that Mits says she really has nice tits, we name her "Ice Cream." He calls her that for his reason, and I say that I call her for my reason which is kind of dumb too, I think it goes well with Christine-Ice cream. We're all dumb.

In the early evening, just after supper, Mr. Miyasaki scurried by to say good bye. He got his orders to go to a road camp. But he's not going to go! He earnestly pleads with Mama to understand that what he's doing is right. He talks hurriedly, pleadingly. She is sorry. What about his missus and the children and the old woman, his own mother. He clasps her hands in his and looks downcast for a moment, and then he straightens up and says he has to go. *Nigen naran:* must run away! And he's off. Look after your mother, he whispers as he gives me a hug. We follow him with our eyes as he joins up with his friends waiting under the trees of the Grounds, and they go through that passageway across on Cordova Street and disappear. Miyasaki-san!

Monday, April 13, 1942 - There's a letter from Papa for Mama when we get home from school. It's of course in Japanese and she tells us that he's fine and that he's living in a bunkhouse with all the other men and that he's working, going from camp to camp setting up small bath places, fixing pots and pans, fishing, meeting friends, enjoying the vast Rocky mountain scenery. He likes the family photo, thinks we all look fine and well. The other day someone took pictures of the work gang and he'll send them along when they're ready, and pictures of him and Jiro-san, too.

Aunt Kinue, Papa's youngest sister, and her two young kids are going to go to Strawberry Hill and joint Jiro-san's family, now that Mr. Teramura, her husband is out in the road camps, too. Kinu-chan, as Mama calls her, came to Canada in 1940. she is one of the last to come from Japan, but as it happens she was actually born in Canada and was taken back to Japan as a baby. When she arrived in Vancouver at that time, she had to stay in the Immigration Building for a few days. I don't know why, but I do remember going down to the CPR docks and to that building and looking up to see this woman dressed in Japanese kimono waving to us from behind the barred window. Probably the very same window I was looking up at a couple of Sundays ago. And when she was released she was in our house dressed in the fine kimono and I had never seen any one like her before. Miyo became very much attached to her, and she would go around after her, calling: Kinu-chan, Kinu-chan. She of course didn't speak any English at all. Aunt Kinue, Oba-san. So she and her two kids, cousin Keiko and baby Takeshi, are going to Uncle's farm. He wants to look after everybody. In Strawberry Hill.

A strange air is settling down on Powell Street. Streets are deserted, stores are boarded up: on the block next to ours, T. Maekawa, the big clothing store has all its front windows papered over and Shibuya's across the street has wooden screens fixed to the windows from the inside. Other stores are screened over, covered up, boarded up. Powell Drug Store is open. Of course, it's owned and operated by Mr. Shaw. The other day, Mits and I wandered down to the Japanese Language School on Alexander and looked the place over. On the west side facing the playground and Jackson Avenue, the glass panes of the big windows were nearly all smashed. We threw a couple of stones ourselves to hear the crash and the tinkle of broken glass.

Wednesday, April 15, 1942 - Tak came by to say good by. He's leaving for the road camp tomorrow. It's our turn now, the Niseis Oba-san, Tak says. *Taka-chan, Taka-chan, ki o tsukete ne,* Mama keeps on saying; please look after yourself. Mama wrings her hands in the folds of her apron and goes off into the kitchen for ocha, tea. Don't bother, Oba-san, Tak calls after her, but she is not listening. Tak fidgets with his hands and arms, rubbing his muscles up and down: let's write to each other Spike, he says, we'll keep Ted, the postman, busy. Sure, I reply. I really want to.

Later, Scotty and Rinzo come over and they sit around the cold, old stove in the shop. Tak moves about restlessly about the now empty shop. Only a couple of large crates and the counter at the front remain. Bill Kilby had taken the canaries, so there's no more chirping from the birds. Tak doesn't like what Scotty and Rinzo are saying. They're saying the won't go. They haven't got their orders yet, and both are eligible and liable, but, no, they're not going to go. It's not only that their old man is dead set against their going, and he for no other reason except to be contrary to the government no mater what, but for Scotty and Rinzo, it's just what the hell, why should they have to go anywhere?

But there's something else, maybe. Rinzo is a keen student of Japan, the culture and history and language, so it's kind of expected that he would be against Canada and for Japan, but what did that have to do with his determination not to go? Tak has no argument to make, he's saying he's going to go despite everything because it's expected of him. I don't follow any of the reasons, by Rinzo and Scottie or Tak.

I walk up with Tak along the Jackson Avenue side of Powell Grounds; the chestnut trees are full and green and huge. I walk with him all the way over to his house on Cordova Street. We didn't talk much. At his place his mother is very nice to me and so's his younger brother Terry. A neighbour of theirs, Aki Okawana is there, and of course, I've known her a long time. I know her from Strathcona, she's in Mits' class, and we've been through kindergarten and the United Church Sunday School together. We are childhood friends. And Aki's talking about Ted the postman and how nice it is that there is such a good person among the hakujins. Aki talks a mile a minute and she's a lot of fun, I mean I laugh at whatever she has to say. It's the way she says it. Do you know what a good person is, Hide? she asks, and answers it herself, well, a good person is someone hard to find. Tak gets up to go. He gives me a hug, I bury my head in his shoulder. Tak goes out. He's going to his girl friend's, says Aki. Bye, Tak. I get up to leave for home. Aki says, don't forget to come by to say good bye if you're going anywhere, Hide. Sure, Aki, bye! Thank you, Oba-san, 'bye, Terry.

Friday, April 17, 1942 - Scotty and Rinzo are in hiding. Somewhere. No one is saying anything. Old man Amemori is proud of his boys, but Mama says it's on his urging that his sons have decided not to go to road camp and gone into hiding. Kaz is flitting about so I'm sure he knows where they are and is in touch with them. Bringing them news and food and cigarettes. I convince myself that that's what he's doing. It sounds all so tense and exciting.

And then just after supper I strapped on my roller skates and went down Dunlevy Street. Below Alexander is quite a nice downhill ride, and I wanted to get some of that. As I got to the foot of the road, the railway crossing bell started clanging and the guard rail started to come down. Hooray, a train's going to pass. The steam locomotive is the big one for the CPR Transcontinental. I wave at the engineer. He indulgently waves back. Then the tender, the mail-car, baggage cars, passenger cars, and best of all the dining cars, and then more passenger cars, and at the end the club car with the observation platform. It turns the bend and is gone. I look at my watch. I've got time for another go down the hill. When I'm half way down the bells go again. Hooray! Another one. This time, though it's a freight train. Nothing wrong with that, the game here is to count them. Make a guess about the number two passenger coaches, real old ones, and on them are Japanese men. Wow! I can't recognize any but I wave and wave, both my arms! They wave back and I can see that some of them are shouting. But the windows won't open. The faces are piled up three, four to a window. And then the caboose trundles by, and that's that. The brakeman leans out hanging on to the sidebars. It's been quite a week.

Tomorrow I have to go down to the waterfront beach and start gathering driftwood for the kitchen stove. The sawdust bin is getting empty and Mama thinks we should start storing firewood. What I'm to do is go down and find driftwood and bring them home on the wagon and cut them up with a hand-saw and chop them up and get them ready for the kitchen stove. We have one with a sawdust burner attached to it, but now of course with all the commotion there's no one making deliveries of anything, least of all sawdust. Mits has to do the same thing. So we agree to go down together.

Saturday, April 25, 1942 - I did a really sneaky thing today. I hit Isamu

Kitamura when he wasn't expecting it, I mean I surprised him and hit him with my fist and gave him a bloody nose. It's just before supper, Shoji and I have just stepped out of the baths and are standing by the washing machine watching the towels spin. Through the peeling strips of the painted glass window of the door I see that Isamu is about to open the door. Quickly, I step up, open the door and let him have it. Blood spurts out. I yell at him, you lay off my kid brother! for that's what provoked it. He had made Shoji cry over a game of marbles, and I was not going to have any of that. I guess I hit him quickly like that because he's a bit bigger than me, and I was just acting up. Shoji is startled. I grab him and say let's go, and leave Isamu with blood streaming down his chin. An hour or so later, after supper anyway, I'm in Mrs. Kitamura's Nabata taxi office saying I'm sorry I went and did that. She had phoned Mama about the incident, and Mama in no uncertain terms made it clear to me that I was to go over and apologize to Isamu and to his mother. Otherwise, she'll take me over to Kitamura-san herself. I go by myself to speak to Isamu's mother. She asks me why do I do such things, you are such a quiet, studious boy. I squirm about with no answer to offer. It's true I've hardly ever been in a fight. What was I trying to do by hitting Isamu like that?

To change the subject: down in the low tide beaches this morning the Kawamoto brothers were out looking for driftwood, too. The brothers out there were Henry, Kirk and Roy. Tom, the father. Anyways, they were looking for lots of wood because their mother is running the manju works and the shop is still operating. They had a big wagon. Hank and Kirk wear chink pants, black cotton high-waisted pants with bell bottoms and two rows of open fly-buttons in the front. They're called chink pants because they're hand made by fast Chinese tailors down in Chinatown. Cost four bucks. Mits wants one right away. When you got your money, Hank says, we'll take you. Through the afternoon we hang out together and are joined by Butch Inamoto. They all have bikes, CCM with V-handles. We figure we're like a gang. Butch and Hank are the oldest, they must be at least 17. They've both quit high school. They say they just want to loaf about. They're always hitting each other in the biceps. Hard, too!

Butch has a sister who used to be in my Japanese school class. Her name is Sally. The Kawamotos live on Cordova near the corner, next door to the funeral home, and right across from Powell Grounds. In baseball season balls hit into the right field have been known to land in their front yard. Of course, then it's a home run. The manju store is right next to Fuji Chop Suey House on Powell Street. In the shop's backyard they have a huge pile of wood, and several cases of empty bottles. That's Kirk's main activity, getting and selling bottles, liquor bottles and pop bottles.

During the week I had a card from Tak in Yard Creek. Not much happening here, he writes, and nobody's working hard. The food is good and the scenery is wonderful. Wish you were here, and so on. I think of Christine in Hastings Park only a street car ride away but already like another planet, another world. We'll go there next week.

Friday, May 1, 1942 - Yesterday Mama caught me reading a book behind the counter in the shop. I should've been at school, not playing hooky like this. She's furious. I run all the way to school, and get a lateness pass and join the class. A simple thing, skipping classes, but Mama was simply furious. What did I have in mind? Nothing. I just wanted to curl up somewhere and read a book. Disappear from the world. Doesn't everyone feel like that sometimes? Today when I got back Fu-chan was visiting Mama. They were so deep in their talk that they didn't hear me come in, and I sort of stood by the doorway and saw them sitting in the kitchen. Maybe Fu-chan was crying, she turned her face away when I was noticed. I said 'hi' and I dashed out.

Later I hear from Mama that Fu-chan and her family, that is her husband, Mr. Tamaki and their 2-year-old, and the rest of the Tamakis, are all going to work on a sugar beet farm in Manitoba. My, what a big country this Canada is, she says. It can be so troublesome when a country is this big, she adds. I don't know what she means by that remark. But I think I know what she means when she says we will have to get ready to go at a moment's notice. I've seen her sorting out her personal things and clothing and all that. We might be on the move. Tomorrow, Saturday, Mits and I are going to Hastings Park. We plan to leave early in the afternoon, so we're going to have all the morning things done. Get the wood, I mean. I'll get Shoji to help. Today I got two cases of empty orange crush bottles from old man Amemori and got 50 cents from the

Men's dormitory Hastings Park (photo courtesy of City of Vancouver Archives)

Fukushima's Milk store at the corner. I can buy something for Christine, I think. Counting everything I got $1.25, a small fortune, I think.

Sunday, May 3, 1942 - I'm taking today to write about yesterday. The

day started out swell, sunny and all that as we gathered driftwood. But it was showering by the time we got to the Hastings Park Manning Pool, the official title. We took the Hastings streetcar and got off as we would if we were going to the fair at the main entrance. No guards; we slip in and run for one of the buildings. Inside, we're hit by the sound. What a noise! It's like a roar, a steady roar. Like at the Orange Hall boxing nights, between the fights. Papa took me last September. We don't know what building it is, but it's filled with iron bunk beds, rows and rows of them, draped over with sheets and blankets and quilts and clothes and curtains, and filled with women and kids, kids like us and younger, and babies, babies, toddling about, all crying. How are we ever going to find her in this mess?

We step out at the nearest exit. In the next building, we find that it's for men. Here too, rows of bunks, some with men sprawled out, dead to the world. Not as noisy. We walk through an aisle. In an open area a table is set out, men are ringed about it, a card game is in progress. Dollar bills are flying about. Real money. Further down, young boys are playing the same game on a bunk bed. With pennies and nickels and dimes and quarters. Real money. We stand about and watch the play for awhile. Mits thinks he wants to join. I nudge him so that he could see that one of the boys has his shoes and socks off and picks at his feet as he plays. We move on. And then by good luck we bump into Sam Sonoda. Sam from Woodfibre. He's ashamed of it but here he is, he says, had to move in, there was no where else to go. Gee, I wondered where you'd gone to, I says. He tells us all about the awful food and stomach cramps and the diarrhoea. And then he tells us a funny story about the school at the Park: the principal, a man named McRae broke three sticks whacking the hands of twenty boys in grades seven and eight. Their crime: they refused to open their mouths to sing at a school concert. They certainly "sang" at the punishment. Finally, I ask him about the Uno's. Sure, he says, they're here. All hometowners kind of keep in touch with one another, more or less. The Missus is kind of sick and Christine, too. She's in the infirmary. Where's that? What's wrong with her?

The sun's out when we come out again. Sam shows us where the infirmary is. We can't get in for a visit or anything. We both want a glimpse of her. We walk around the building. It's a low building, there's a semi-basement area. If we go down to the bottom we won't be able to see through the window, we'd be too low. If we stay where we are, on the rise, we could catch a glimpse, a partial view of a big clinical room. We can make out an activity: women and girls in housecoats, dressing gowns, white shifts, are being examined by a nursing team, one of whom is tapping the naked backs of the women. Mits and I hunch down in silent awe at this spectacle. Suddenly one of the girls being tapped is Christine, Mitsuko, Ice Cream. We whistle and call out her name. They all look up at us, startled. We wave at Ice Cream. She recognizes us, slips her shift back on, and waves at us. Her smile! The curtain is drawn. Show's over, but we have seen Ice Cream!

After that we swank about, looking it over as if we owned the place. Out on the fringe of the place a high wire fence separates the Park from the public golf course outside. There a group of young boys, like us, are jeering-cheering at a foursome of women golfers. They look great, these women in their slacks or plus fours, and shirts and short sleeves, and they play on with calm disdain of their audience. On the other side, the Happyland is wide open but nothing is working. All the rides, the merry-go-round, Shoot-the-Chute, the Giant Dipper are still, some are covered up. Kids walk around distractedly. We go over to the grandstand and sit up in the high seats and watch the ships in the inlet. In the near distance is the Second Narrows Bridge with the folding span in the middle. It's turned out to be a great day. We look for Sam again, and find him; leave with him the things we got for Ice Cream. Mine is wrapped and tied up.

It's a book. I'm giving her my copy of "How Green Was My Valley". I'm sure she'll like it.

Tuesday, May 5, 1942 - We hear today that Rinzo and Scottie were caught by the Mounties just yesterday. At Main and Hastings, of all places. That's broad daylight. What we're they doing around there? I asked Kaz, what happened? He says how should I know. Those shitty, shitty Mounties. Amemori-san walks about stunned. And Amemori-no-oba-san sits by the darkened table. Haru-chan comes over to talk and cry with Mama. I take Shoji with me to the bath house behind The Sister's Cafe. Only a couple of men are there in the tubs. We don't know them. It's early. We laze about in the medicine tub. Suddenly a whole bunch of guys, all strangers to us, come in. They are loud and boisterous. Steveston types. We get up to leave the tub. After towelling ourselves, I notice my watch isn't where I think I put it in the open clothes locker. It's gone. Someone must have taken it, maybe by mistake. I ask everyone there. No one knows anything. Getting dressed quickly I go to the front and ask Hori-no-ob-san whether anyone may have returned a watch he took by mistake. What are you saying, she asks. I tell her again, maybe it was one of the two men who was there with us. He may have taken my watch by mistake. She says she knows them, one of them lives over the pool hall at Sun Rooms. Pool Hall? I have a flash that one of them is the tight-suited dresser who told Hats and me to bugger off once. Yeah, that's the guy. I'm convinced. But now I have to go home and tell Mama. Shoji trails after me as I hurry home.

Mama listens to my story. How stupid can you get, just letting everyone see how you look after your watch. Not putting it in your pocket. She's getting worked up. We're going to go to this man's place right away and get it back, she says. He'd better be the man you think he is. I hurry to keep up with her. We get to the Sun Rooms. Her simple plan is to knock on every door. We climb up the stairs and start at the top floor, the floor above Hats' place. The very first door she knocks at is quickly opened and it is the tight suited man. He opens the door wider. He has on the very same suit. Mama politely but firmly explains why we are here: she says my son says that you may have mistakenly taken his watch this evening at the *furo-ya*, the baths. If so can we have it back, please.

Nani, kono yaro! What, this little kid! Saying that about me. That's a like! This is a very serious matter to insinuate on me. He spits out his words. Mama shrinks back. I cower in fright. She apologizes for her mistake, our mistake, and grabbing my arm and bowing many times to him, hurries down the stairs and out of the place. It's dusk. Heedless of anything, she clutches my arm firmly and rushes me home. Once there she flings me under the kitchen table. Oh, you made any awful fool of me, she pants. *Yaito da*! I grovel and cry under the table. I don't want yaito, I don't want that kind of punishment. It's burning moxa on your bum. No yaito, no yaito, I cry. She pulls at my legs, I kick and try to pull away. She is down on all fours, she has the lighted moxa in her hand. I kick and scream, kick and scream. My pants are pulled down. I cry in pain, in anguish, I don't know. It's over, she sets me free. I hurry to my room and throw myself on the couch, exhausted, panting, I fall asleep. Hours later I get up and write all this down. I am keeping a diary.

Saturday, May 9, 1942 - Miyo says she's never seen Mama like that before. Who has? I ask. Shoji and Sumi were terrified, they say. So was I, I say.

Yesterday evening I'm sure I saw Scottie and Rinzo on one of those trains. I was on the embankment at Dunlevy, above the tracks and was moving down towards the passing train when I caught sight of them. I was positive it was them. And today Kaz said, yeah, they were on that train, They're being sent to a place called Angler, he said. It's like a prison camp. And now from a railway siding in Hastings Park people are being sent to places they call "ghost towns" with names like Sandon and New Denver. Hank and Butch are on the top of this kind of information.

I've taken to hanging about with them a lot. Just being with them. Hank takes me on his bike the way Tak used to, riding side saddle on the frame. Mits has his own bike. Me, I can't even ride one. They are all going to show me one day. Late this afternoon we climb up onto the roof of the Hotel World by going up the fire escape iron stairways at the back. Top of the world. Nobody knows we're up here. We throw pebbles down on the tin roofs of the sheds of Sun Peking Chop Suey House next to the hotel. Two Chinamen come jabbering out the backway and look up and down the alleyway. They never think of looking up. Who would? We can see that they are laying out sheets from a dough which is flattened out by a long paddle. One end is fixed and the cook bounces up and down on the other end, and the dough gets flattened out. The other guy has a long knife and is slicing up the flattened dough with a similar kind of motion of the knife. There you have your fresh *yet-cha-mein*. We send another pebble down to the tin roofs. *Rat-tat-tat-tat*. And another: *rat-tat-tat-tat*. Shouts from below as we hug ourselves and stifle our laughter.

And then on the other side, the Powell Grounds side, Hank spots what he thinks is a Mounties' car. It's a tan Chevrolet, 1939 model. He says he's certain of that because the other day a guy stepped out of this car, a big guy. A copper you know for sure, came up to him as he was sitting out on the steps of his place, and asked if anyone else besides him was at his house. Hank said, nah, no one, and the guy went back to the car. The guy had a brown suit on, and the driver, a navy one. Mits is dispatched to see if that's the car by checking out the occupants. Get the license number and don't give us away, Hats says. Mits hurries off. We are into real adventure. Roy is dispatched to get some Coffee Crisps and Coca Cola. We are at war. The army needs to be fed. We continue to survey the world at our feet. Mits returns. Yeah, that's them. He has the number. Roy gets back, and we munch on chocolate bars and pass the bottles back and forth. We can warn the guys say Hank, the guys who are on the lam. We just have to find the guys so we can tell them what's happening and let them know when the Mounties are around. Okay, Butch is to go by the pool halls and look dumb, and Spike, you are to go and talk to your pal Kaz and find out a few things, if you can. I clamber down and run home to see if Kaz is around. He's not, but Bill Kilby is visiting. He's heard from Papa, and his letter said he might be coming back for a little while, maybe in a mouth or so. Bill asks me what I'm up to, and I say, nothing much. Mama says I'm looking after a lot of things, getting the wood and things like that. But he's lost his watch, she adds. I flush at this and back away, and run.

But no Kaz. I run back to the rooftop. No one's there. Guess they all had to go. I sit by the ledge and look over to the mountains and the ships in the inlet, and the trickle of traffic down on the streets. I think about the trains and run down Dunlevy. Down at the corner of Powell, just past the beer hall, I stop for a moment to watch the judo guys flexing their stuff at the judo-ka. The windows are wide open, and their *kiais* can be heard out in the street. Three pair of judo-kas are slamming each other down on the mats. Thud, splat, thud, thud, interspersed with the cries. An older man with a goatee also in judo uniform sits impassively off to one side. Above and behind him is a framed calligraphic writing in broad strong strokes of some ten or so kanji characters. It is flanked by photographs of judo men, portraits and group pictures. Down on the train tracks it's only the Continental gliding by this evening. There are some other people looking around expectantly. I spy Kaz. I walk home with him. He does not know anything. Just that Scottie and Rinzo were with some friends at that time. It was in Fairview. That's not our territory.

Sunday, May 17, 1942 - A whole week went by like that. Mama hears that Mr. Miyasaki has been caught, and that Oba-san and the boys have been caught, and that Oba-san and the boys and the grandmother are all going to move into Hastings Park. And it's said that everybody, but everybody, is going to be moved out. Place names are getting familiar: Kaslo, Greenwood, New Denver. Some people who can afford to are moving on their own, to Taylor Lake, Bridge River, Lilooet, Christina Lake. Mrs. Oya, upstairs, helps Mama sort out the real information from the rumours.

On Thursday the leaders of the gambari-ya group were caught in a couple of the rooms in Patricia Hotel. Geez, that's right near the Kawamotos, on the corner of Hastings and Dunlevy. Hank shakes his head in powerlessness. He thinks some one squealed. Not the hotel people, what do they know. It's an inside job, he says, there are collaborators, inu, dogs, he says. He's heard about them. Some of them are judo-kas, other are well known guys like that Asahi baseball player, Frank Shiraishi. I stare in disbelief. I don't understand. To protect themselves they go and finger other guys, he explains. so they could stay on in Vancouver, so they don't have to be shipped out. But, I say, everybody's going to have to go; that's what I heard. Yeah, Hank says, sooner or later. It's Saturday, Hank and I are sitting in the Sister's Cafe, waiting for the others. I'm spooning up a dish of ice cream. Chiyo has been nice to me, patting my back and scruffing my head. She's done this ever since the wrist watch business. I squirm happily. Eddie, Flo's boy friend, studies the menu on the juke box. Gene Autry is singing:

South of the border, down Mexico way,
that's where I fell in love
when stars above came out to play,
and now as I wander,
my heart ever strays,

south of the border, down Mexico way.
Ai ya ya ya yai, ai ya ya yai.

I think of Christine, Mitsuko, Ice Cream. Next Saturday, I'll go to see her at Hastings Park: see her, and Freddie and Richard and Sam. Hanks moves over to the juke box and jokes about Ed, shadow boxing around him. Ed laughs and slaps the juke box. Chiyo boogie-woogies by herself to the "Chattanooga Choo Choo." I see all this in the mirror behind the counter, and see myself looking.

Thursday, May 21, 1942 - On the way home after school, I'm coming down Jackson Avenue, just after Hastings when out by the alley way in the vacant lot next to Harry's Cleaners I see a couple of guys sitting about under the bushes. I get closer. It's Joe Akiyama and Peanuts Koyanagi. They are looking uneasy. I say don't worry, I'll keep a look out. They're waiting for Frank, Roy's brother. They've been doing this for a couple of weeks now they say. I ask if I can help. Thanks, but we've okay. Don't tell anyone you saw us, Spike; this from Peanuts. Next time you see me I might be a chink, he laughs, I'm fed up with being a Jap.

Sunday, May 24, 1942 - Went by myself without Mits yesterday to Hastings Park. It wasn't hard to find Christine. I saw Mieko and she led me to her. She was sitting outside in the sun; there was some one with her. A guy, older than me, a guy with a white shirt and an ascot. A guy smoking a cigarette. She scrambled to her feet and drew me aside and tried to be nice to me, I soaked it up as much as I could but it was no use. Finally, she said she'd like to spend the day with me but she's already made promises and you know how it is. And, oh, yes, thank you very, very much for the wonderful book. I really, really enjoyed it. I threw the tufts of grass I've been grabbing and said okay and got up to leave. She said she'd be at the Graduation Day Ceremony at Strathcona, in June. I'll see you there then, Okay, I said, and left.

Then I went to look for Freddie and Richard and found them outside the Women's building. Eddie Morita was with them. They were all looking pooped, sprawled out on the grass. Seeing me they all got up and we ran around down to Happyland and the Grandstand and acted like apes with Richard as Tarzan, and ended up lining up for supper which was beans and wieners and bread, and then I left them and the Park. I walked home through the alleyways, below Powell Street. The street lights were on by the time I got home. I said to Mama I saw the Miyasaki boys but not Obasan. Tomorrow's Empire Day. It used to be the day for Maypole dancing and sports games at Strathcona, and the events would be held on Powell Grounds. It used to be a big day. Not this year, not any more.

Monday, June 1, 1942 - Last Saturday Mits and I found ourselves down at the Japanese School. Between what is the new building and the old building where there are some classrooms and where the teachers, some of them, used to live in the upstairs quarters, we found a door with a broken glass window. Some one had broken in.

We tried the door and it opened. We wandered in and looked the place over. It was all messed up. All the desks and seats were gone, some of the blackboards pried off. And in the upstairs area, it was just rubbish on the floor. In the kitchen a can for *senbei* crackers stands in the middle of the floor. We pulled off the tin: inside was just a mouldy, dusty remains of a bread loaf. What really impressed me then was that the teachers used to eat white bread. I remark on this to Mits. He says, so what, everybody does. The mouldy dust gives me the spooks. I say let's get out of here. That same afternoon we break into Nabata's Shoe Store. From the alleyway we find a narrow, narrow space between the two buildings and we squeeze ourselves through it and find that at the end is a window on the ground level, a small window. We push it and it opens inwards. We slide in and find ourselves in the basement stockroom; there's enough light to look about. Shelves and shelves of shoes, all kinds. Feeling tight and crazy I take a pair, just any pair, and say let's go. Mits has a pair too. We clamber out. Over at Kawamotos we call out Kirk and Hank and show off the shoes. They are men's black leather oxfords, expensive looking. No good to us says Hank, too big, but we can sell them. Where? Over on Main Street there's a shoe store. They'd be glad to see these, say that our big brother bought them but now doesn't want them. Has to leave in a hurry and will sell for a reasonable price. Hank says he'll do it. Off at this store we wait for Hank across the street. In a few minutes he comes over with a big grin on his face. Sold them for three bucks each, he says. Mits says he wants a pair of chink pants. Okay we can go and order them now, says Hank. You? he asks me. No, I don't want any pants. Let's all go to a movie, I says, the Beacon. The best seats at 50 cents. And we do all of that. On the screen is "Desperate Journey" with Errol Flynn and Ronald Reagan, a war adventure about three Allied soldiers escaping from a German POW camp, and then a vaudeville show. So that was Saturday. And then on Sunday, I find that the Yamashitas have moved into the church on the corner of Powell and Jackson, the United Church. The minister, Rev. Shimizu and his family have been shipped off to Kaslo, and the Yamashitas are in the apartment behind the church. There's been no services for quite some time. I know the Yamashita boys, Bruce, David and Gordon from Sunday School days. Their father operates a rooming house way down near the Mc & Mc's. He's an elder of the church and they've moved in because the rooming house has been closed down or something.

We fool around with a basketball in the gym. We have the run of the place. But we don't go into the church part. Later we play penny-ante poker in one of the meeting rooms. There's a stack of Bibles in the corner.

After school today, Monday, we did that again. Played poker in that room. This time Roy Miyasaki and Yoshimi Kinoshita, his buddy, joined us. It's getting to be a big table.

Wednesday, June 10, 1942 - Lots of small stupid stuff. Mits and Roy continue to get into that shoe store and now Butch is into selling the shoes to stores, even second hand shops and junk stores and to people out in the street, on Hastings. I look along the alleyways and poke about people's garbage. Found one good book, a beautifully bound volume of verses: "Palgrave's Golden Collection of English Verse," and a pile of Doc Savage pulps. Exam time at school. I'm just getting barely through, I know. I feel it and don't care. My favourite subject is history; I really like it, but now I don't care how I do in the exam. I'll just sit through it.

Friday, June 19, 1942 - Graduation day for the Grade Eights at Strathcona. In the auditorium we are singing "Will Ye No Come Back Again" when I turn my head and look up at the balcony and see Christine. Gee whiz! And then the graduating class sings:

We are leaving Strathcona,
We are the graduates ...

and I sing: we are the evacuees... And then outside in the sunshine, but she is engulfed by all the others.

Saturday, June 20, 1942 - Let me just come to an understanding about yesterday at school. It was, I think, one of the nicest moments when we all sang "Will Ye No Come Back Again," the song about Bonnie Prince Charlie leaving Scotland for good after his failure to win the throne of England for the House of Stuart, him being a Catholic and all, and after Culloden and all that. You can imagine his people on the seashore waving farewell as he is rowed away towards the waiting ship, and maybe they're singing this song. In any case there's that famous painting I saw somewhere in a history book, and it's always on the program at these graduation ceremonies at Strathcona. But when we were singing it yesterday, I knew it was for us. Are we going to come back here, not to Strathcona, but here? Here? Am I? And then when I saw Christine up there in the balcony, and saw that she saw me, I just felt that "here" was just now, only "now," as I sang that song, as "we" sang that song, and I felt so big yet so light, and I floated up and filled the auditorium. And then the graduating class sang their song: "We are leaving Strathcona, we are the graduates..." to the tune of a drinking song! And that was that. And later, trying to catch her for myself, but she is surrounded; I went home kicking a can.

Life Magazine has a special feature on that battle of ships and airplanes in the Pacific, the Battle of Midway, the papers called it. The fate of the world is being battled out somewhere, but our gang, Hank, Butch, Kirk, Mits and me, we played out our knife games on the evenly groomed lawn of the funeral parlour. We all have pocket knives now, from the shoes, and we play games like this: longest blade of the knife is cocked out and right angles to the handles and the tip is stuck into the ground, and then it is tipped over at the handle end with a finger or the hand and flipped into the air, and if it lands after a couple of somersaults with the tip once again sticking into the ground, that's the winner. The best ones are those that have the most somersaults, the most turns of the flipping.

Then there's one with the open knife; the tip of the knife is held tip down on certain parts of the body, like the head, the shoulder, the elbow, and the knife's end of the handle part is held by a finger: the idea is to let the knife fall with a little flip of the finger and stick itself into ground. The winner is the one who can stick the knife into the group sequentially from all those prescribed parts of the body.

And then there's the final one where one hand is splayed palms down on the ground with the fingers stretched out, and the trick is to stick with the other hand the point of the knife blade between the fingers, with each alternate jab being the base point of the knife blade near the wrist, and this as fast as possible. So, you stretch out your fingers on the ground, the knife point is stuck by your wrist and you jab it in the space between the thumb and the forefinger and back to the wrist area, and on to the space between the forefinger and middle finger, back to the wrist area and so on. And the fastest one is the winner. Mits is the fastest one at this most dangerous game. He does it in just a couple of seconds. Nervy Mits. And with the right or the left hand, too.

And then Butch pedalling up the avenue, spots some guys coming down the iron fire escape at the rear of the Hotel World and realizes that there are some guys holing up in there. How about that? Right under our noses, he exclaims. Let's find out who they are.

Swinging up on our bikes we cut them off at the alleyway leading out to Gore Avenue. Turns out that they're from Fairview and Kitsilano, and they're young, just a couple of years older than Hank. There are four of them here talking with us, but inside the hotel they figure there must by maybe about twenty or so all told. The guy who's doing most of the talking, this stocky looking guy, his name is Tammy. He's saying that he took the position that if there's going to be any kind of mass evacuation it has to be on the basis of all the families together. That's what his old man maintains, and that's his belief, too. His father, though, has already been picked up, he says. Hank wants to know how that's going to keep the family together. Tammy kind of bristles at this and spits out, you gotta stand up for what you believe in. And moves to go. Hey, we say, we want to help you guys. Maybe, maybe, Tammy says, and is already going. His buddies follow him. One of them is up ahead, looking up and down the avenue. A wave, and they run across the street.

We decide to check out the hotel, find a way to get inside and see what's what. Up on the roof top if one of the skylights can be opened, we'd be inside. Taking extra care, we go up on to the roof and try the skylights, everyone of them. None will open up no matter what we do. The glass windows in iron frames are corrugated with wire meshes, and no matter what we do we can't get them open. None of the fire escape doors will open. On the street level, looking casual about it, we try the main doors and basement windows. No luck. The ground floor used to be occupied by a Japanese trust and savings company, like a bank. Well, that's tightly shut up, with all the fixtures still in place, as if it were a Sunday. And there are other small offices on the Dunlevy side of the building and, of course, they're all shuttered and closed up tight. We leave it at that and head for home, except Butch. He wants to hang around and see who's going to turn up. He ducks down by the seating stands of the ball ground which is directly across from the Hotel World.

Monday, June 22, 1942 - Sunday was a real Sunday. Nothing happened. I took Shoji down to Jimmy's Island down at the other end of the Old Hastings Mill, past a small refinery. It's a sort of a built-up place with a circular concrete wall and an earthy mound in the middle of it, and it must be about thirty feet across and there's a small tree and a bunch of bushes growing on it. It's only an island when the tide is high. Never found out what it was for, not that there's anybody around to ask, although there is the National Harbours Office just at the head of the entrance to this whole area, after you cross the railway tracks. I guess you could ask there, but who would want to. They're like government people, they're like cops: some of them wear uniforms.

Jimmy's Island. You could dive off on the inlet side, and there's a diving board of sorts out that way, but the best is just to be in swim shorts and soak up the sun. Which we did. I'm not much of caught up with the Australian crawl, in this one you keep your head down for six or more strokes without turning your head to gulp in air, and of course you kick like hell. But the way I learnt how to swim is the good old sink-or-swim way. It happened two summers ago right here at Jimmy's Island: a guy named Tak Ozaki and another guy threw me into the water from the pier. Up to then I'd been sort of dog-paddling about near the beaches and not getting anywhere. Getting thrown in like that meant I just had to sink or swim. Simple. Maybe that's why I don't care too much about swimming.

Tak Ozaki is the guy who used to take me to school when I started in Grade 1; he was then in Grade 8. He's a nice guy. Like Rinzo he refused to go to road camp and was picked up. And last year before the war, his big brother who went to Japan to enter university killed himself because he failed his third entrance examinations. It really impressed Mama: it is so difficult to get in but once you do, it's easy, life is easy; but when you fail and fail and fail, it must feel that there is no other way out. She said this to a very quiet Papa. The Ozakis are family friends, they have a noodle and sushi restaurant on the ground floor of the apartment building owned by Dr. Uchida, just a few doors away.

At Jimmy's Island, just a couple of young white guys were around, guys who don't know how to swim, they just splash about. Never seen them before. Mits joined up later but we didn't do too much. Shoji went home on his own. On our way home Mits and I duck down by the refinery to see if there's anybody on that small secluded beach out front. Yes, there's a white couple there, young. She's wearing a white two-piece suit and he's wearing skin-tights; they're lying on a towel, sunning themselves. They can't see us, we're above and behind them, on a pier. We sit on our haunches grasping our knees and watch. Nothing happens: they pull out a cigarette each, light up and smoke. They don't even touch each other. We get up, Mits throws a stone into the water to startle them. We move on. It was a Sunday.

And today Mama said Papa is coming back for a few days. Maybe next week, soon, soon. And then he's going to go to a camp and build a place for all of us, Papa and many other men. A new town. All this is breathless. Wow! Where are we going, what's happening? And Papa coming back. Where was he all this while? I missed him but didn't miss him. He just wasn't here. But now. He's coming back. Papa.

Friday, June 26, 1942 - School is finally over. In our class Michiko Ishii made a little speech thanking Miss Bolton for every little thing that she had done for the class and for someone like herself. I felt very tight while she was speaking and felt very relieved when she finished. Michiko Ishii on Miss Bolton. Miss Bolton, she who used to say "Made in Japan!" whenever a thumb tack broke under her thumb and then turn and glare at the class, and I used to think, at me; Miss Bolton, the tall and stiff and forbidding teacher in her steely rimmed glasses, this Miss Bolton, Michiko Ishii really liked her.

Our class president Evelyn Chin also said something. A lot of faces were missing. Of course, Christine's, and Gabby's and Hats' and Victor's... there were new faces in their places with names I didn't pay attention to. And then Miss Bolton wished us all good luck and hoped that we would all be back at Strathcona in Grade Eight, come September. We are leaving Strathcona, we are the evacuees...

Before supper time, whip over to Kawamoto's. Nothing's happening, I mean no one's been able to connect with any of the guys on the loose. And after supper, we're all down by the railway tracks, and this time a whole bunch of people on the embankment. It happens that a full train load of people are going to a ghost town, Sandon, and they are mostly Buddhists from the Vancouver area, Fairview and Kitsilano, New Westminister and Marpole. It's said too that this train will then stop at the siding in Hastings Park and take on more coaches loaded with evacuees for Sandon. I guess we all wait about a half hour or so, and when the train comes, the small crowd surges out almost to the tracks and some in the crowd cry out as those on board are recognized. The open windows are crammed with faces. People run alongside the coaches calling out names and shouting farewells. As the last coach passes they come onto the tracks waving and waving. Suddenly Mits breaks out into the front and runs madly after the train, leaping and hopping. Some people in the crowd urge him on, others laugh. Mits is a crowd pleaser all right.

Sunday, June 28, 1942 - Saturday, down by the waterfront for driftwood, hauling it back home, sawing and chopping it into firewood. No Mits. Later, I go by his place, just along the alley. Their place is getting closed up. Everyone is by. I ask his mother for Mits. *Mitsuru ka*? Is he here? *Inai*. He's not. I pass by Powell Drugs, and he's there loafing. Wanna come to see the Mummy? I says. I know he's never seen it. What mummy? Where? I'll show you, I says. At the center of the domed room, the museum, a glass case mounted on a platform table encloses a clay casket, and inside this is the mummy, Egyptian. It is said to be that of a young boy, and I guess that's why the fascination for me. A young boy, three thousand years old; a young boy wrapped in linen and preserved I don't know how. A young boy who didn't grow up to be a man even though he's been around so long. The empty black eye sockets, the wrapping clothe material like sheets of spider's webs, the complete and utter look of antiquity about it, wow! I look up to smile at Mits. See, I say, the mummy. He finds it spooky. Remember the moldy dust of a bread, he says. Subdued, we climb down the staircase.

Out on Hastings and Main, we watch the traffic. Suddenly, Mits says there's the Mounties' car. It's a tan Chevy sedan, all right, but as it passes by we can see that it isn't. Not by the driver, nor by the look of the car. That whole business has shrank almost to nothing. Must mean that most of the people have been picked up. We certainly didn't do much for them, though Hank and Butch claim that they helped out on their own when we weren't around. Like keeping a lookout for some guys a couple of houses down from their place, getting smokes and stuff. But not for the guys who were supposed to be in Hotel World. According to Butch nothing happened that time he kept watch, not a thing. Nobody came, nobody went. Guess no one was there.

It's Sunday, today. Nothing much today. Joined Bruce and David over at the church for card games, and invited Kaz to come along. We play low ball and high ball, low tow and high tow (best five out of seven, betting on each card), five card stud: dealer's choice. We pinch the card to take a peek, and live and die for the inside straight. Kaz hauls out a package of cigarettes. Sweet Caporal. We smoke and choke. Time flies. Won more than fifty cents. Kaz more than sixty. Losers were Bruce and David and Yoshimi Kinoshita.

Friday, July 3, 1942 - Papa's home! He will be with us until Monday. When he picked up Sumi, she cried; she had been hanging back behind Mama and must've been startled. But it was all right for all of us after that. It's been four months since we were last together, all of us. I guess we've grown, but Papa hasn't changed much. He smokes a pipe now, though, a Dunhill pipe with Edgeworth tobacco. He looks tanned and fit. How was the fishing? Oh, lots of small mountain trout, brook trout, got the cook to fry them up, he says. Shows us pictures of him with some of his work mates; in one of them, Papa holds the fly rod in his hand. Another one, with a lot of men standing in rows, and sitting in front amongst them, a hakujin man and two hakujin women, one blonde, one brunette. I look up at Papa, I would like to ask him who are they? What are they doing up there? But I don't.

He has a souvenir for me, a small nicely made picture frame; made out of yew and hemlock, he points out. It is all neatly pieced together. Made by a friend in the camp. I look for a picture to put into it and find one in a magazine. A photograph of Nelson's ship, Victory, in the Thames. Mama sends me out to get special food stuff from Maruno's Union Fish Market, next to Maruchu's. Ask for any fresh fish, she says. She says that Maruno's will close down this week, and then what?

After an early supper we are taken down to Sumiyoshi for the last of sundaes of anything they might have. It's a reunion for Papa with some of his friends: Blackie Sekine, Ichii-san. We leave Mama and Papa there and head back home ourselves. On the way back I pop into Sister's Cafe and announce to everyone there my Papa's back home. Everyone there turns out to be just the sisters, Flo, Chiyo and the youngest one, May, and Ed, and skinny Georgie-Porgie. I do the same thing at Horizon, the general foods and dry-goods store, two doors down from us, and Frank responds with a hooray. Here they are down to the family as the work staff and even Misao who was in both my school classes is tending the store. They are just about the last grocery type store that's open. Frank asks which camp are we going to, and I say according to Papa a place called Tashme. Oh yeah, that's going to be out somewhere near Hope, says Frank, they have to build it from nothing. Papa says he's going there to help build it, I add. Right, says Frank, gotta make lots of stove pipes, and then he asks, Do you know how they get that name, Tashme? No, I say. Well, says knowledgeable Frank, it's from the first two letters of the last names of these big shots who run the Securities Commission: Taylor, Shirras and Mead. TA-SH-ME, get it? Where are you people going, I ask. We don't know yet, he says, we just don't know.

Sunday, July 7, 1942 - This morning I see Mama and Papa together in their bed for the first time. I must have seen them in their bed together many times before, but I have not seen them as they are this morning. Yet though I have seen nothing, I am struck by something that I know I do not know. In the kitchen I see a package of cigarettes. I draw one out and changing into my clothes, I duck outside and have a smoke on the flat rooftop of Amemori's unused garage, overlooking the alleyway and beyond. From where I stand I can see clear through to the front of the Japanese School on Alexander Street and that's because there is a vacant space between the houses, a no-man's land. On one side is the fenced up house and property of the Izukawas, owners of Burrard Fish Company; the house is heavy, imposing, and the wooden fence is high, maybe ten feet. The house has been vacant since mid-May, when the Izukawas moved to Christina Lake. On the other side is what is called a "long house," with the balcony walkway of the two stories on the open side reaching all the way from the alley to the street beyond. It has one or two-room "cabins" which used to house people who didn't seem to work all day, bums and rubbies. Rough-looking white guys, and sometimes women. It used to be that it was kind of dangerous to pass down this vacant lot; there would be men sitting around a small fire heating up Sterno cans and the place would be littered with small empty bottles of various extracts. We knew they drank these things instead of alcohol because they were cheaper. The people then looked meaner and rougher, but there was one guy we named "Popeye" who looked like Popeye talking out of the side of his mouth, and he was kind of fun and friendly, trying to scare and tease us. From where I stand now, I would crouch down and watch them until they saw me and called me out.

Now there's a whole different kind of people living there, younger looking and healthier, anyway, and I guess they're all working in North Vancouver shipyards or in some war effort. I can see a couple of guys now, sitting on the railing, another sauntering about on the walkway, taking some air. The whole place looks cleaner, although the junk in the jungle is still there. Papa asks me later what kind of *itazura* (mischief) did I get into. I say really nothing, Papa. I had my watch stolen. He grunts, and then: *Shiyo ga nai na, shiyo ga nai yatsu da na*. Can't do anything about that, eh, and, can't do anything about you, eh?

Friday, July 10, 1942 - Today, Mits and his family left for Bridge River. They are going to a self-supporting settlement, which means they're going to be on their own. The whole family, together. Mama says, "*Yappari kane mochi da ne*, they were rich after all." Actually it came as a surprise to me; Mits didn't say a word about this. I guess he was reminded to keep quiet about it until everything was set. I went by their alleyway door to see them leave; a moving truck was there. They were taking a quite a lot of stuff I thought. Trunks and cases and crates and clothing bags and suit cases. They were going down to the CPR Station to join the other families leaving for the same place and for the other place, Lillooet.

I say good bye to the Tanakas, Bill and the sister, and tofu-ya no ojisan, oba-san. And Mits. He promises to write. He's wearing long pants and white shirts, he looks clean. He's not his usual ratty looking self, in short pants. You look good, I kid him. See you around, he says. And then Mama says Aunty and George and Ian and Yuri are going to Vernon in the Okanagans, the apple country. Uncle Jiro is already there. They are going to take the train at the New Westminster, maybe tomorrow. And Aunt Kinuye and the kids are going to Sandon. When are we going, I ask. Mama: "*Sore wa Wakaranai*, that we don't know."

More changes: The Oyas upstairs are going to move downstairs to Papa's tin shop and a family of hakujins from Saskatchewan is going to live upstairs in their apartment. The two pianos, Naomi's and Miyo's, are moved out for safekeeping somewhere, arranged by the Oyas, maybe the same place where the radios went. The Amemoris stay put, so too the Horizon folks next door. The Wakabayashis moved into Hastings Park. The Yamashitas to Kaslo. What about the Kawamotos? At the manju shop at the back I am surprised to find a man chopping wood who is, it turns out, the old man of the family. Just because I had never seen him nor heard the boys talk about him I had assumed he was in the camps somewhere. I ask after the boys: he replies in English, out, out on the beach, getting wood. But he says, Kirk in the Japanese way, *Ka-ku*. I think about going down there but turn around and walk along over to the Hatanakas, way down on Cordova, Tak's place. The place is empty, vacant. Wonder where they went? I could go across the street and ask at the Okawaras, but I don't. I head for home. I tell Mama about the Hatanakas. Yes, she says, she's heard that they went to Slocan last week.

Sunday, July 19, 1942 - The Homenchuks moved in upstairs on Friday. What a big family! Not counting the parents, Mama thinks there are fourteen children. I think twelve. Oya-san says thirteen, from 9 months old to the oldest girl, 19, and there are four boys and nine girls all told. Mr. Homenchuk is a war worker in the shipyards at North Van. They are Ukrainians, she says. Today, I got to talk to one of the boys about my age; his name is Frankie, same as his father, he says. They come from the prairies of Saskatchewan but they left it nearly a year ago. Came to Vancouver where there's work for the father and the older girls. They're all war workers in some factories, the girls; and the father is on night shift in the shipyards. He takes the ferry to the work place everyday late in the afternoon and returns early in the morning while everyone's still asleep. There's a sign put up over the door to their place. It reads:

QUIET!

War Worker

On Night Shift

When school starts Frankie thinks he will get into Grade Seven. All the moving about, he says, ever since they left the Prairies, mean that he got behind. He's going to catch up, 'cause you got to have your education. Frankie is a serious looking one with dark blonde hair and a quizzical look about him. He brings out a kite, a small red triangular one with a long tail, but there's no wind coming up. It's not too good during this time of the year, I tell him. In the Fall when the wind is strong and steady the place here, the Powell Grounds, would be full of people flying their kites, I tell him. Big ones that take four people to handle them, big square ones designed in Japan, I tell him. Not to be outdone, he tells me that he used to fly kites a mile high on the Prairies. What are the Prairies like, I ask. It's flat flat flat and you can see far far far and the sky is big big big, he says, proudly, and the wind blows blows blows.

Monday, August 3, 1942 - Everything seems to be on a standstill for us. Nothing is happening and no one really to be with. Butch has been gone for a long time now, he went to Slocan. And Hank and Kirk are keeping to themselves. No sense of doing things with anybody. No more top of the world from the Hotel World.

This morning, Frankie tells me about how they used to have a giant bow and arrow sort of thing out on the Prairie. He thinks maybe we can make one, too. The bow should be made from a flat iron brace, he says. We go down to the Canco looking over the junk next to the machine shops. It's an aimless sort of moving about, we get tired of it. Do you want to go to Kitsilano Beach? What's that, he wants to know. I explain: it's a nice sandy beach, we just take a street car ride, it has the best chips in town, lots of salt and vinegar, it's fun. The fact is I haven't been there all summer at all, not once, and, before, like last summer, it was the place to go. If it wasn't Kitsilano, then it was out on English Bay with Freddie and his pals. We get out to Kits, we have our swim tights on under our pants so we don't have to go into lockers to get changed. We'll wear them wet or dry after. On the beach, the crowd isn't that big at all. The tide comes in around mid-afternoon, and then you can roll and swell with the waves as you swim from one large resting raft to the other. It's not deep either. So it's okay. But Frankie just wants to wade out to the first raft and stay there, more or less. He jumps in the water and climbs back out and calls it swimming.

After the swim, we wander over to the pool. I know I'm doing all these things because Frankie is with me. Alone, or even with Mits, say, I don't think I would want to be out here now. It's a funny feeling. After all, we're being moved out because they don't want us here. I don't bother trying to explain all this to Frankie. We get the chips, they come in paper boxes, they're small and almost crispy and hot. Lots of vinegar and salt. Then we stand under the outside shower and wash the salt water off our bodies and hair. We wait for the swim suits to get nearly dry, and then slip on our pants and head for home. Kitsilano and English Bay, Freddie and Richard: how we used to argue whether the chips were better at this place or the other. Did it ever matter, and all the sand castles and forts that were built. Jericho Beach and Spanish Banks!

In the twilight we're back. We had walked from Main Street. We drop in at the Sister's Cafe. How about a soda pop? On the juke box a Japanese record: "*Shina no Yoru*," (China Nights.)

Minato no hikari	The lights of the harbor
Murasaki no yo ni	In deep purple
Yu re ru rantan	The swaying of the lanterns
Yu me no yo.	Like a dream.

Monday, August 10, 1942 - Trekked over to Hastings Park to see Freddie and everybody off. It's down at the railway siding, early evening. Freddie, looking every jaunty, has a baseball cap on his head. So they're finally off, Freddie and Richard and Ken and Oba-san and grandmother Obaa-san, for Slocan. They've had only two letters from Mr. Miyasaki, from Angler; it's an internment camp with barbed wires and guards and everything, Freddie says. And where they're going to, Slocan, it's right by a lake, it's in the Kootenays, a mountain country. Freddie is excited.

The siding is crowded with people all milling about; the train is ready and waiting, almost impatiently. Up in the front the locomotive huffs and puffs and its bell keeps clanging. There's been almost one trip a day from this place, each with more than six passenger coaches. Freddie says they've made a lot of friends here but their Mom is glad to be getting out. Really glad. He's glad too, to be moving on. The Park was just crazy. Mrs. Miyasaki says she will never forget the powdered eggs and powdered milk. I say that's what the people in England eat too. She makes a face.

People are now crowding aboard the train. Men with armbands shout and lead the way for others. They must be those war vets from the First World War now working for the Commission as security personnel. Oba-san is helped aboard by one of these men. Freddie and the boys get an open window. There's no platform at this siding, so the windows are up high. We strain to talk but it's no use. There's not much to say. Freddie throws me an orange. Thanks, I peel it and eat it up just like that, without thinking. Then the train is moving. I stand where I am and wave. When the train goes around the curve it will be running pretty close to the Giant Dipper, the roller coaster of the Happyland. Now that's a ride.

I walk back home along the alleyways. There's a knot of people walking along together like this. We stop at each street and look up and down and then dash across. A couple of girls are talking very excitedly as they walk. I don't know who they are. Before seeing Freddie off I had gone about looking for Christine. Christine! Not a word from her. In the Women's building, I went to the place where they were quartered, her mother and her sister, Mieko and herself. There was another family there this time, and one of them said, the Unos went off last week to the ghost towns. Where? Don't know, maybe Tashme, maybe Slocan. Maybe Tashme.

When I get back Mama is still up; I say I went to see them off. Mrs. Miyasaki said, *Mama ni yoroshiku*, best regards to your mother. Mama says ah, Hastings Park. Over by the racing track at Hastings Park, the horses are running every afternoon.

Tuesday, August 18, 1942 - Took Frankie to see the school. He knows where Strathcona is but not the layout of the school. So, I said let's go. There's the old part and the new part, the inside and the outside; that is, the old building is right in the middle and the new ones have been built up around it. It's not that big. On the Georgia and Princess side of the corner, there's a small baseball diamond, and the ground has a small pebbly surface. But in the middle part, it's asphalt, great for marching about, I says. I show him where my home room was, out in the front facing Pender Street. And then we sit around by the flower beds, and then Frankie asks the strangest thing. He asks me if I knew anything about the rape of Nanking. Sure, I says, the Japanese soldiers did that in China, yeah, it's a Chinese city, they burnt it and did other awful things. I know nothing about that, it was 1937, yeah.

Well, Frankie says, my Pop saw a newsreel film (he says it, "fi-lum"), about that at the place where he works, the Burrard Drydocks. Yesterday, they showed the film, and the American guy who filmed it was there in person to talk about it. Pop was just disgusted by the whole thing, he says. It was just awful what those Japs did, his Pop said. Never see'd anything like it, his Pop said. Just butchering people, his Pop said. Those Japs must be goddamn awful, his Pop said. I look at Frankie, I don't know what to say. I mean we're just hanging around together. The war past and present has been very far away these past few weeks or months. I don't know what to say. I guess your father got mad, eh?, I venture. He didn't stop talking about it, Frankie says, he just kept on going on about it. All the men at the shipyards were hot about it. They're going to show the film again later this week, maybe in every work place. What about the Germans, I say, the Nazis? And the British? Just a couple of months ago, didn't you hear about those giant allied bombing raids on German cities. Those 1,000 plane raids? They're meant to kill people, not just soldiers. Which side are you on? Frankie demands. The Allies, I say. But I don't like what I'm saying, and I don't like what we're talking about.

I get up abruptly and walk away. Frankie trails behind. At the corner were abreast again, and we run across the street. Later when no one's looking I tear down that sign which says: Quiet .... War Worker, etc. I know Frankie's old man is going to raise hell. What am I doing? Who cares?

Wednesday, August 19, 1942 - And today more war business. Dieppe. Canadians raid Festung Europa. The newspapers are full of it. Lot of Vancouver soldiers in the attack. I see Frankie heading off somewhere on his own. Don't see him at all for the day. Old man Homenchuk, his Pop, I guess. The sign is back up, and he didn't make a fuss.

Saturday, August 22, 1942 - Horizon's. Frank Hori treated me to a movie today. Went to see Bud Abbott and Lou Costello in "Pardon My Sarong" at the Vogue, down on Granville. Fatty and Skinny are all right, but I like Stan Laurel and Oliver Hardy cut ups much more. Afterwards we walked through Hudson's Bay and David Spencer's, two big department stores, just gawking.

Frank is full of gossip and information and rumours. Did you know, he says, there are now only 6,000 Japanese left in Vancouver, and most of them are in Hastings Park. And did you know, that a young guy, 22 years old, was arrested because he wasn't registered? They mean business, these Mounties, these government types. Did you know that Bill Tanaka lost his cherry to the youngest of the Sister's Cafe? And did you know that Eddie, Flo's Eddie, goes around beating up the *inus*, the collaborators? And every time he does that, he slips on his black gloves. Did you know that? Did you know that there are still more than 50 ganbari-yas jailed in the Immigration Building? And don't you want to go and see Ina Rae Hutton when she comes to town next month with her hot shot all-men band? Wouldn't you just? And wouldn't you know that just about everybody skipped town without paying their bills. Now, that's not being Japanese, is it? And did you know that Mr. Kawamoto is a Great War vet?

We end up at the Sisters' Cafe for soda pops and ice cream. You know, he finally says, we might be going to Regina. Uncle is going to open a lingerie shop. I'll get to work in the shop: lingerie, women's undies and pajamas, nice silky things, he says. All smiles. Regina? Yeah, Saskatchewan. It's okay now, the Depression is over, the farmers are going to be rich. The war is not going to end just like that, you know. People who had to leave, like your Homenchuks, I guess they had it real hard; I guess they lost the farm can you imagine the drought year after year and all that dust blowing about; and then they had to move into a town and then the city and finally here. And now it's the war, it's come at the right time, sort of rescuing them. Funny, eh? In Regina he can finish his high school and even go to college, Regina College, and then get into the business world; Frank muses. I say that I admire the way he has it all worked out. Let me tell you, Hide, he says, as long as there's a movie house or two, I'm not going to bitch too much. But listen, he adds, there's one movie we must see, "This Above All" with Tyrone Power and Joan Fontaine, from the novel by Eric Knight, it's coming soon to the Plaza.

It looks like the Sisters' Cafe is not ever going to close up. The juke box is crooning away a Japanese hit from the Thirties:

Ah, Shanghai no, hana uri musume... Ah, the flower selling girl of Shanghai...

Flo and Chiyo dance together. Powell Street casaba, Frank murmurs. I can suddenly see how really shabby the place is. A mirror down one side of the wall, with glass shelves and glass cases, shelves for glass cups and bowls, cases for cakes and donuts and pies; below that the ice cream and pop coolers and the work counter, on it toasters, coffee urns, cutting boards; then a gas stove with skillet top, I don't know, your usual worn out cafe equipment, crusty and not too well looked after; and then the counter on which we've been served, enameled how many times over on the top and on the front side, with crummy chrome banded spinning seats raised up on a platform six inches off the floor, not too well looked after; and then, on the other side more shelves up against the wall and these are wide wooden ones, holding any manner of things, from school supplies like scribblers and pencils and crayons, to old Vancouver souvenirs, like the Coronation and the Golden Jubilee, and shoe laces and envelopes and letter paper in boxes, and more boxes with you know what else; and on cup hanger hooks screwed into edges of the shelves and brackets, Ex-lax and Aspirin packets braced up in cardboards are holed up, and many more things besides, and other punctuation: graphics and pictures from calendars and a framed photo of Fujiyama; further down then, in front of all this mosaic of shelves and bric-a-brac, big glass counters with mirrored sliding doors in behind, and on these shelves Japanese dolls, O-himes in brocade silk kimonos and porcelain figurines from mythic stories, and abacus boxes, and other cheap Japonica. There are two sets of wire ice cream parlor tables and chairs, and by the far end of the glass cases, the juke box, a fat Wurlitzer with juicy lights and fat sounds, lit up like Mecca; behind this, a small round table with couple of chairs: a place to lounge for the sisters and their friends, and on odd occasions, a place to sit and smoke for their mother, *Ofuro-ya-no oba-san*, a place for her to watch the world.

She sees us now, in earnest conversation, Frank Hori, Hiroshi-san, talking, me listening. It's the Japanese sandman, calling us to the land of sleep and dreams… It's Chinatown, my Chinatown, when the lights are low …. It's twilight time on Powell Street.

Tuesday, September 1, 1942 - Schools starts today, but not for us. We've heard from all directions about the fact that there's no school for Japanese kids. We heard it all last week. But today just because I know that school is starting, I feel hurt and left out. I see Frankie going with some of his brothers and sisters. Out in the back I look over to the Japanese school and see a soldier with a rifle on guard at the entrance. I call over Kaz and together we cut through the jungle junk beside the long house to see what's what. It's nothing much, the soldier is there guarding the place because overnight it's become a special Canadian Army training center. That's what the sign says. We want to know what kind of special training but think that if we ask we would be considered spying so we say nothing. Even when a Vancouver Sun reporter suddenly swoops down on us and asks us for our views about what we see, we say nothing. We act stupid. We are, in fact, stupid.

The guard snaps to attention as a brown military car comes and an officer gets out. The reporter hurries in after him. We survey the place, from the Jackson Street corner. All the window panes are back in place. I tell Kaz about busting some of them. He laughs, he did too. On the other side, the older wooden building has been scrubbed down and painted, it looks good, all white and clean. Next to this former school building is an old rooming house, run down and dilapidated and everything else. On the door of this place a sign has been posted by the City Health Department. It says that the building has been condemned because its unfit for human habitation. Not two weeks ago the place was swarming with people.

Cheerful Ted the Postman has a letter for Mama from Papa, nothing for me, one for Miyo, from Grace Kanda in Lemon Creek, and a couple for the Oyas. Ted the Postman banters about with Mrs. Oya about the City Council and its tussle with Ottawa about the chlorination issue, whether the city water should be treated or a resolution to Ottawa saying that Vancouver does not want Japs in the city after the war: the Japs should be banned forever; the Japs should be sent to Japan.

It is looking to protect the future, my future, remarks Ted the Postman sarcastically, who got those bastards in there anyway? Ted the Postman, ginger-haired, skinny as a rail and just as tall. He knows just about everybody. He should, he brings them all their mail. He knows we are leaving soon. Are you folks ready, he asks, for Tashme? Ready or no, we're dying to go, I say. Just dying to go. Bill Kilby calls to say he's coming by. I'd answered the phone and I report to mama. He wants to make a final agreement, she says. When he comes over he's in the uniform of an ambulance driver. That's my job for the duration, he says. I'm with the Kingsway Ambulance Service. So, it's all been agreed that he will look after us by taking us down to the station on the day of our departure. All of these things were worked out when was back here briefly during July, he says. You must remember to tell your Dad, there's nothing to worry about, and he remembers, oh, but he will have them by now. He's talking about Papa's machinery and tools stored away in a warehouse.

Kilby: Yes, he's going to have his own sheet metal shop in the camp. And I told him then that I will come and see you folks. And I will, for sure, it's a promise. We see him off in his black Dodge ambulance car. It has a siren mounted on the front fender.

Thursday, September 10, 1942 - Our departure date is set, it's September 17th, a week today. We will be taking the CNR train at the Thornton Station near Cambie Grounds. It's the nicest train station in town, set in its own parkland, not like the CPR station which is in a warren of piers and warehouses downtown. We're leaving! Mama sets about getting rid of the last of our things, things we can't take by hand. Like the sofa and tables and chairs and drawers and chests and kitchen things and the washing machine and the stove and the beds. And all the other things, but I don't know what. I am not there when these things happen, she looks after it all. I don't even think of saying do you want me to help. I take it for granted, I take everything for granted. That it will all be okay simply because she is looking after it, or Papa, or someone is. A very poor attitude.

I think back to the yaito moxa incident over the wrist watch. I really haven't gone over any part of that time, or that incident. I just let it pass by me then. Sure, for a few days after I smarted, and felt injured, and maybe even bruised. But even then I didn't want to think about it. And never for a moment did it occur to me to see it from her side. We never talked about it at all. Now I think it over and I recall the words she was spitting out at me at that time: *Ha kaii, ha kaii! Shaku ni sawaru! Shaku ni sawaru!* what she was spitting out, and what those words mean, was: My teeth itch! My teeth itch so much I want to claw at them! and, my spleen, the spasms touch my spleen! Words that are words that come from deep inside, expressing deep anger and frustration. I will never know what really brought them on, perhaps she herself will never know, too. I'm sure it wasn't just the watch. I got over what happened, step by step, and I can't make it out. What did I do!

And during all this time Papa was away in the mountains, and when he came back for the couple of days in the summer, was he here at all? And now since two months we last saw him, we're all going to be together again. The whole family again. Did I miss him while he was gone all these times? I guess so, but how was he here for me before all these happenings? And what's happened to Joe Akiyama, and all the Akiyamas, and Peanuts Koyanagi and Sockeye Tsukamoto. And Taka-chan? I just wonder and don't ask, for who can I ask?

Wednesday, September 30, 1942 - My first entry in Tashme! And we've been here already two weeks tomorrow. But let's begin on the day we left Powell Street. Our train was for eleven o'clock in the morning, so we were up early and had breakfast with the Oyas. They had makeshift arrangements in Papa's old shop. Miyo and Naomi, Ida and Sumi were so excited they could hardly sit still. Kaz from the next door came and went, and Frank Hori from Horizon, and later old man Amemori helped with the last of the packing, roping up suitcases and clothes bag. And I tied and retied my small bag. And then Bill Kilby came, smartly dressed in his ambulance driver uniform and cap. And he came in a Packard, a Packard with the top down. Is this the car that the King and Queen were in? Bill Kilby laughed, sure! And we piled in and rolled majestically down Powell Street. We were going at last! Good bye! Good bye! At Thornton Park we rolled by the exact spot where Miyo and the Murakami girls and a hundred others dressed in kimono waved at the King and Queen in 1939. Miyo says, Gee willikers, do I remember that! I'm positive the Queen smiled at me.

At the CN station, it's one big noise and confusion, but with Bill Kilby's help we find ourselves in one of the coaches and our stuff is piled in. And then Bill Kilby has waved good bye and the train is pulling out. The coach is crammed, every seat is occupied, and the aisles are jammed with suitcases and things. I look about to see who's with us and there's Aki waving frantically at me. She comes over and sits with us. Turning to Mama, Aki says, *Ii ne, oba-san*, we're all going together, isn't that nice! We cross the Fraser at New Westminster and we're rolling down the valley as we bring out our sandwich lunches. Oya-san made these, I say to Aki and add: oh, yeah we were driven down in a Packard by Bill Kilby, Papa's friend, with the top down. Oh, aren't you lucky, Aki says. And then later she brings back a round tin can and opens it to show a round pound cake. "You know who baked that? Ted the Postman's wife," Aki asks and answers. We laugh, and we all have a piece of the cake.

At Hope, we get off the train and pile into open trucks. It's fourteen miles to the camp. It's early afternoon and hot and dusty. In the direction we are to head into, the mountains just seem to jut up. The road is through a narrow mountain valley, but at one point it ascends on a curve, and at the crest of the curve a wide vista opens up and a broad valley is revealed below, stretching out flat towards the mountains at the far end. I think of Ronald Colman approaching Shangri-La for the first time.

We arrive; we are met by Papa, and it is dust and wind and confusion, and note there's a bonfire on which a mattress is set to burn, and a man with a big stick is whacking at it and crying out: *Nanking mushi, nanking mushi* (bedbugs, bedbugs). I didn't know what it was. And then we stumble into our quarters, a tarpaper house, freshly built, and we have a new address, 316 Third Avenue, Tashme, B.C. Outside, all around us, a clamour of pounding hammers and shouts of men as the work of building a hasty town goes on. Two days after that I am sick and lying in the wooden rack of a bed with straw ticks for mattress and I am throwing up until I can throw up nothing but bitter tasting bile, and I have thrown up on Mama I don't know how many times, and I sweat in a fever and it lasts for a day and a night. And then I am well. I had heaved myself inside out.

Around us a ring of mountains. An inverted bowl. A world upside down. I read Omar Khayam, from my Palgrave's:

And underneath this sheltering bowl
We call the sky,
Do not lift up your finger;
For It moves as impotently as you or I.

I have new friends now, too. Mitsuru and Seiji Tahara, two houses down. Mitsuru, another Mits. They're from Ocean Falls. And Hats Uchida, he's here, and he knows them, from Ocean Falls. And the Uno's are here too. Christine! I saw her at the post office. As they say, never in a dream. She asked, are you still reading a lot? And I said no, but would like to. And then she said, too bad, there's no school. And then, we exchanged addresses, and then we said, be seeing you. And, that's it. But she's here. I can't believe it.

And of course Aki is here, too. She sees me down the street or on the boulevard and cries out: Hide, Hide! And maybe I'm going down to the bathhouse waving a towel, and I hear her calling: Hide! She's funny! They live way at the end of the town, the last house on this side of Tenth Avenue. Our house on Third Avenue is made up of four small rooms and one common room for cooking, eating and living. We occupy three of the rooms 'cause we live in this house with another family, the Shishidos, a family of three. Oji-san, oba-san and Kenny, a three-year-old. Oji-san is a lumberjack, an old pro with bowlegged legs, and he is old; oba-san is soft and pretty, and she is young. I think about what Taka-chan used to say about arranged marriages, marriages of convenience: no love, no hope of it ever.

I wonder what brought them together. I wonder about my wonderment, and remember the time in July when Papa was home from the road camps. I am not over that sight of seeing them together in bed, Mama and Papa, for I am afraid that I am not a child of love, and I do not wish to find out about it at all. But I am bound to them as only a first born can be, and I am reminded of this by the very form of address that others, relatives and friends, would make: *chonan*. And I want to know about their early lives, Mama and Papa, their childhood and youth, and all the things that made them move to a country like this, and I want to know more than I can ever know want to know. And I want to know because there is no one who can tell me.